## hampstead theatre

## THE REP
Birmingham Repertory Theatre

HAMPSTEAD THEATRE AND BIRMINGHAM REPERTORY THEATRE COMPANY
PRESENT THE WORLD PREMIERE OF

# The Maths Tutor
# by Clare McIntyre

Cast (in order of speaking)

Anna  Sally Dexter
Tom  Nicholas Figgis
J. J.  Ben McKay
Paul  Christopher Ravenscroft
Jane  Tricia Kelly
Brian  Martin Wenner

Director  Anthony Clark
Designer  Patrick Connellan
Lighting  James Farncombe
Sound  Gregory Clarke

Casting Director  Siobhan Bracke
Deputy Stage Manager  Maggie Tully

Press Representative  Charlotte Eilenberg
charlotte.eilenberg@dsl.pipex.com

**The Maths Tutor** was first performed at Hampstead Theatre on 25 September 2003 and at The Door, Birmingham Repertory Theatre on 4 November 2003.

The text that follows was correct at the time of going to press, but may have changed during rehearsal.

# The Company

### Clare McIntyre  Writer

Currently unpublished work includes **Beware of Pity**, adapted from the book by Stefan Zweig.

Theatre work includes: **The Changeling** (Graeae Theatre Company at Sadlers Wells Studio); **The Thickness of Skin** (Royal Court Theatre); **No Warning for Life** (Women's Playhouse Trust); **My Heart's a Suitcase**, for which Clare was awarded the Evening Standard Award for Most Promising Playwright and the London Drama Critics Award for Most Promising Playwright (Royal Court Theatre also Japan); **Low Level Panic**, which received the Samuel Beckett Award (Royal Court Theatre also produced around the world at Liverpool Playhouse / Royal Theatre, Northampton / Lyric Hammersmith / Italy / Sydney / Australia / Andrews Lane Theatre, Dublin / LA Theatre Artists, California / Barrow Theatre Group, New York); and **I've Been Running** (Old Red Lion Theatre).

Television and film work includes: **Eastenders, Hungry Hearts, Low Level Panic, Castles, My Heart's a Suitcase, Junk Mail** and **Hi How Are You**.

Radio includes: **Noisy Bodies, Shelf Life, The Art of Sitting, Walls of Silence** and **I've Been Running**.

Clare has also had an extensive career as an actress in theatre, film and television. She was diagnosed with MS in 1996.

### Sally Dexter  Anna

Theatre includes: **The Lion, the Witch and the Wardrobe** (RSC / Sadler's Wells); **Macbeth** (Queens Theatre); **Closer** (Society of West End Theatre Award and Olivier Award nomination), **A Midsummer Night's Dream, The Recruiting Officer, Entertaining Strangers, The Winter's Tale, The Tempest, American Clock, Dalliance** (Society of West End Theatre Award and Olivier Award), **The Threepenny Opera, Love for Love** (National Theatre); **Oliver** (Society of West End Theatre Award and Olivier Award nomination, Palladium Theatre); **Desire Under the Elms** (Watford Palace); **The Duchess of Malfi** (Bristol Old Vic); **The Devil and the Good Lord** (Lyric Hammersmith); **Gentleman Jim, It's a Madhouse, A Man for all Seasons** (Nottingham Playhouse); **Once Upon a Mattress** (Watermill Playhouse); **A Midsummer Night's Dream, Twelfth Night, The Swagger** (Regent's Park); **Lady Betty** (Cheek by Jowl); and **Don Juan, King Lear, Troilus and Cressida** (RSC).

Television includes: **Family, A Touch of Frost, Night and Day, Tough Love, Psychos, Playing the Field, Roger Roger, Hamish Macbeth, Wing & A Prayer, Have Your Cake, Deacon Brodie, A Few Short Journeys of the Heart, The Plant, The Act** and **Sam Saturday**.

Film includes: **Paradise, Firelight, The Final Curtain** and **Wittgenstein**.

CDs include: **The Karma Sutra, Songs from Thomas Hardy's Wessex** and (soon to be released) **Loud and Low**.

## Nicholas Figgis  Tom

Nicholas trained at Drama Centre London where he won the Lawrence Olivier Bursary in 2002. This is his first professional role for the theatre.

Television includes: **Byker Grove** and **Our Friends in the North**.

## Tricia Kelly  Jane

Recent Theatre includes: **Barbarians, Dancing at Lughnasa** (Salisbury); **The Inland Sea** (Oxford Stage Co.); **Some Explicit Polaroids** (Out of Joint, UK, European and US tour); and **Local** (Exposure season, Royal Court Upstairs). Also: **Julius Caesar, Ion** (RSC); **King Lear, Not I, Sunsets & Glories, Two** (West Yorkshire Playhouse); **Seasons Greetings, A Whisper of Angels Wings, Julius Caesar** (Birmingham Repertory Theatre); **Victory, Seven Lears, Et in Ego Arcadia, The Last Supper** (The Wrestling School); **A Wife without a Smile, The House Among the Stars, Court in the Act, The Way of the World, The Cassilis Engagement, The Choice** (Orange Tree); **The Government Inspector, The Seagull, As You Like It** (Sheffield Crucible); **Amphytryon** (Gate); **East Lynne** (Greenwich); **The Voysey Inheritance** (Edinburgh Royal Lyceum); **A Mouthful of Birds, Deadlines, Fen** (Joint Stock / Royal Court); **Juno & The Paycock** (National Theatre); and work at the Almeida, Nottingham, Southampton, Lancaster and many more.

Television includes: **Casualty, High Stakes, My Family, The Bill, Dangerous Lady, Christobel, B&B, This is David Landor, Josie Lawrence Show, In Sickness and in Health** and an **Omnibus** on Caryl Churchill.

Film: **A Small Dance, Real Lies, Big Feet, This is History Gran** and **Top Dog** (Best Short Film, LA Festival 2002).

## Ben McKay  J. J.

Theatre includes: **Secret Heart** (Manchester Royal Exchange); **Romeo and Juliet** (Chichester Festival Theatre); **Hiawatha, Pinocchio, A Prayer for Wings** (Torch Theatre Company); and **age, sex, loc@tion, The Life and Adventures of Nicholas Nickleby** (NYT, Lyric Hammersmith).

Television and film includes: **The Bill, Casualty** and **Watch Over Me**.

## Christopher Ravenscroft  Paul

Theatre includes: **Educating Rita** (Derby Playhouse); **The Woman in Black** (Fortune Theatre); **Absurd Person Singular, The Winslow Boy** (Birmingham Repertory Theatre); **Sitting Pretty** (Chelsea Centre); **Landslide** (West Yorkshire Playhouse); **The Tempest** (Salisbury); **Broken Glass** (Victoria Theatre Stoke) and **Macbeth, The Merchant of Venice, Richard III, Crimes in Hot Countries, Nicholas Nickleby** (RSC).

Television includes: **The Ruth Rendell Mysteries, Midsomer Murders, Holby City, Brookside, The Hound of the Baskervilles, John Halifax Gentleman, Pericles, Secret Army, The Levels, Twelfth Night, PD James' Mind to Murder** and **Coronation Street**.

Film includes: **Henry V** and **Tom and Thomas**.

Radio includes: many plays and readings for cassette including a 9 hour abridgement of **The Aeniad**. Christopher also gives recitals with the English Piano Trio.

## Martin Wenner  Brian

Theatre includes: **The Increased Difficulty of Concentration** (Gate Theatre); **Emma** (UK tour); **Pride and Prejudice** (UK tour); **In Touch** (Belgrade Theatre, Coventry); **Wicked Games** (West Yorkshire Playhouse); **Out of Order** (Churchill Theatre, Bromley); **Bajazet** (Almeida Theatre); **Sisterly Feelings** (Bromley / Windsor); **Macbeth** (Contact Theatre); **Ring Around the Moon** (New Hebdon Festival); **Under Milkwood** (British Council European tour); **Rough Crossing** (Chester Gateway); **Room at the Top, The Winslow Boy** (Nottingham Playhouse); **Revelations, Forty Years On, The Merchant of Venice** (Chichester Festival); **Intermezzo** (Greenwich Theatre); **Touch and Go** (Croydon Warehouse); and **True Dare Kiss, Command or Promise** (Liverpool Playhouse).

Television includes: **Trial and Retribution VI, Harbour Lights II, Little White Lies, Soldier Soldier, Dearest Pet, Roughnecks, Murder in Mind, Underbelly, Making Out, Madly in Love, Hercule Poirot's Casebook, Anything More Would Be Greedy, Chinese Whispers, Brookside** and **Artists and Models**.

Film includes: **Stealing Rembrandt, Mènage a Trois, Three Blind Mice, Le Blanc aux Lunettes, Wide Eyed and Legless, The Never Ending Waltz, The Russia House, The Rainbow** and **Another Country**.

Radio includes **Afternoon Theatre** (BBC 4).

## Anthony Clark  Director

Anthony started his career as Assistant Director at the Orange Tree Theatre where he directed everything from a schools tour of **Macbeth** to Martin Crimp's first play, **Living Remains**. He spent six years as Artistic Director of Contact Theatre in Manchester where his favourite productions include **A Midsummer Night's Dream, The Duchess of Malfi, Blood Wedding** (Manchester Evening News Best Production Award), **Mother Courage and Her Children, Oedipus Rex, To Kill A Mockingbird** (Manchester Evening News Best Production Award),**The Power of Darkness**, and new plays **Two Wheeled Tricycle, Face Value, Green, Homeland**, and **McAlpine's Fusiliers**, before joining Birmingham Repertory Theatre as Associate Artistic Director. His productions there include **Macbeth, Julius Caesar, Atheist's Tragedy** (TMA Best Director Award), **The Seagull, Of Mice and Men, Threepenny Opera, Saturday Sunday Monday, The Grapes of Wrath, The Playboy of The Western World, Pygmalion, Gentlemen Prefer Blondes** (the play), **St Joan, The Entertainer** and premiere of David Lodge's **Home Truths**. In 1997 he was responsible for launching and programming The Door (formerly The Rep Studio), dedicated exclusively to promoting new plays. The new plays he directed for The Door include **Playing by The Rules** by Rod Dungate, **Nervous Women** by Sara Woods, **Rough** by Kate Dean, **Syme** by Michael Bourdages, **True Brit** by Ken Blakeson, **Confidence** by Judy Upton, **Down Red Lane** by Kate Dean, **Paddy Irishman** by Declan Croghan, **All That Trouble** by Paul Lucas, **Silence** by Moira Buffini, **My Best Friend** by Tamsin Oglesby, **Slight Witch** by Paul Lucas, and **Belonging** by Kaite O'Reilly. He has freelanced extensively including **Dr Faustus** (The Young Vic), **The Red Balloon** (Bristol Old Vic / National Theatre, TMA Best Show for Young People Award), **The Snowman** (Leicester Haymarket), **Mother Courage and Her Children** (National Theatre), **The Day After Tomorrow** (National Theatre), **The Wood Demon** (The Playhouse) **Loveplay** (RSC) by Moira Buffini and **Edward III** (RSC).

This is Anthony's first production as Artistic Director of Hampstead Theatre.

## Patrick Connellan  Designer

Patrick designed **My Best Friend** which played at Hampstead Theatre and Birmingham Repertory Theatre.

Other London theatre includes: **Edward III** (RSC at the Gielgud Theatre); **The Slight Witch** (National Theatre / Birmingham Repertory Theatre); **Paddy Irishman, Paddy Englishman, Paddy...** (Tricycle Theatre / Birmingham); **Perfect Days** (Greenwich Theatre / Wolsey Theatre, Ipswich); **A Passionate Woman** (Comedy Theatre); **Misery** (Criterion Theatre); and **Salad Days** (Vaudeville Theatre).

Other theatre includes: **The Weir, Ham!, The Hypochondriac, Miss Julie, The Blue Room** (Bolton Octagon); **The Rink, A Midsummer Night's Dream, The Dice House** (Belgrade Theatre, Coventry); **Heaven Can Wait** (No 1 tour); **Leader of the Pack** (No 1 tour); **The Marriage of Figaro** (New Vic, Stoke / Scarborough); **Morning Glory** (Birmingham Repertory Theatre / Watford Palace / Cambridge Arts); **St Joan, Julius Caesar, The Atheist's Tragedy, Down Red Lane, Pygmalion, The Grapes Of Wrath** (Birmingham Repertory Theatre); **Coriolanus, When We Are Married, The Rivals** (West Yorkshire Playhouse); **The Wizard Of Oz** (set, Leicester Haymarket); **A View From The Bridge** (Harrogate Theatre); **A Passionate Woman** (Gloria Theatre, Athens); and **A Midsummer Night's Dream** and **She Knows You Know** (New Vic Theatre).

He has also just directed and designed **The Limetree Bower** at the Belgrade Theatre, Coventry and the Edinburgh Festival.

## James Farncombe  Lighting

Theatre includes: **This Lime Tree Bower** (Belgrade Theatre, Coventry); **Making Waves** (Stephen Joseph Theatre, Scarborough); **The Hypochondriac** (Bolton Octagon); **Funny Black Women on the Edge** (Theatre Royal, Stratford East); **Krapp's Last Tape** (Lakeside Arts Centre, Nottingham / tour); **West Side Story, Death of a Salesman, Peter Pan, The Witches, Plague of Innocence, Unsuitable Girls** (Leicester Haymarket Theatre); **Road** (for Pilot Theatre Company, York Theatre Royal / Lyric Hammersmith / national tour); **Beautiful Thing** (Nottingham Playhouse / national tour); **Dead Funny** (York Theatre Royal / Bolton Octagon); **Rumblefish** (for Pilot Theatre Company, York Theatre Royal / national tour); **The Blue Room, The Elephant Man** (Worcester Swan Theatre); **Unsuitable Girls** (Sheffield Crucible Studio / tour) **Amy's View** (Salisbury Playhouse / Royal Theatre, Northampton); **East is East** (New Vic Theatre, Stoke); **On the Wings of a Dream** (Bridewell Theatre); **Hector's House, Women on the Verger** (Lipservice); and **Pendragon** (for NYMT at Akasaka Act Theatre, Tokyo / Yvonne Arnaud Theatre, Guildford).

## Gregory Clarke  Sound

Gregory's sound design credits include: **Abigail's Party** (The New Ambassadors / Whitehall Theatres); **Mum's The Word** (Albery Theatre); **Lady Windermere's Fan** (Theatre Royal, Haymarket); **The Royal Family** (Theatre Royal, Haymarket); **Song Of Singapore** (Mayfair Theatre, London); and **No Man's Land** (National Theatre).

For the Royal Shakespeare Company: **Merry Wives of Windsor** (The Old Vic / Stratford / USA Tour); **Coriolanus** (The Old Vic / Stratford); and **Tantalus** (Stratford / UK Tour).

Other theatre includes: **The Two Gentlemen of Verona, Loves Labour's Lost** (Open Air Theatre, Regent's Park); **Abigail's Party, The Dead Eye Boy, Snake, Gone To LA, Terracotta, Local Boy, Buried Alive, Tender** (Hampstead Theatre); **Semi-Detached, Pal Joey, Heartbreak House, A Small Family Business** (Chichester Festival Theatre); **The Cherry Orchard, Demons and Dybbuks, The Black Dahlia** (Method & Madness); **Nathan The Wise, Song Of Singapore, Nymph Errant** (Minerva Theatre, Chichester); **Design for Living, Betrayal, Fight For Barbara, As You Like It** (The Peter Hall Company Season at the Theatre Royal Bath); **Office Suite, Present Laughter** (Theatre Royal Bath); the new musical **Baiju Bawra** (Theatre Royal, Stratford East); **Dick Whittington** (Stratford East at Greenwich); **Krindlekrax** (Birmingham Repertory Theatre); **The Hackney Office** (Druid Theatre, Galway), **Beyond A Joke** (Yvonne Arnaud Theatre, co-design with John Leonard); and **Dumped, A Midsummer Night's Dream** (National Youth Theatre).

# hampstead theatre

Hampstead Theatre moved into its new RIBA award winning building in February 2003 after over 40 years in a portacabin that was only expected to last for 10 years.

Our new theatre, designed by Bennetts Associates, is home to a fully adaptable elliptical auditorium seating up to 325, and The Space – a studio space for our expanding work with local schools and the local community.

Continuing Hampstead Theatre's policy of producing new plays by both established and emerging writers, the opening season included plays by Tim Firth, Debbie Tucker Green, Stephen Adly Guirgis, Tanika Gupta and Tamsin Oglesby.

'A delight inside: warm, dramatic, visually appealing and imaginatively planned. A splendid home for new writing' THE DAILY TELEGRAPH

Anthony Clark's first season as Artistic Director includes plays from established writers Clare McIntyre, Stephen Lowe and Hanif Kureishi; the second play from the multi-award winning playwright Gregory Burke; an exceptional first play from a young Canadian poet living in London, Drew Pautz; and an original play by Barbara Norden for 7 – 11 year olds and their families – the start of a plan to see more plays for children presented at Hampstead Theatre.

All the plays in the season share a passion on the part of the writers to explore the contemporary world. The writing is inquisitive, imaginative and revealing – trying to make sense of experiences we share while introducing us to new worlds. Qualities that are the hallmark of the commissioning policy of Hampstead Theatre.

# Supporting Hampstead Theatre

## Luminaries
By becoming one of Hampstead Theatre's **Luminaries**, you will be giving vital support to all aspects of our work, and become more involved with the theatre. There are three levels of support and a variety of benefits offered including priority booking, a dedicated booking line, crediting in playtexts and programmes, and invitations to exclusive events. Membership starts at £250 per year.

Our current **Luminaries** are:

### Level 1
Anonymous
Deborah Buzan
Richard Curtis
Frankie de Freitas
Robyn Durie
Richard Gladstone
Elaine & Peter Hallgarten
Lew Hodges
Patricia & Jerome Karet
Richard & Ariella Lister
Tom & Karen Mautner
Judith Mishon & Philip Mishon OBE
Trevor Phillips
Tamara & Michael Rabin
Barry Serjent
Lady Solti
Dr Michael Spiro
Marmont Management Ltd.
Hugh Whitemore & Rohan McCulloch
Dr Adrian Whiteson & Mrs Myrna Whiteson
Peter Williams
Debbie & Derek Zissman

### Level 2
Dorothy & John Brook
Charles Caplin
Professor & Mrs C J Dickinson
The Mackintosh Foundation
Midge & Simon Palley
Michael & Olivia Prior
Anthony Rosner
Judy Williams

### Level 3
Richard Peskin

## Other ways to support us
If there is a particular area of our work that you would like to support, please talk to us. We have numerous projects available covering all aspects of our work from education to play development. As a registered charity, Hampstead Theatre can accept donations from charitable trusts and foundations, gifts of stocks and shares, donations via CAF America or in a tax efficient manner under the Gift Aid scheme. Why not consider leaving a legacy to the theatre to give us lasting support well into the future?

## Corporate Partners
Hampstead Theatre is proud to launch its **Corporate Partners** scheme. This offers a flexible package of benefits with which you can entertain your clients, promote your business objectives and take advantage of everything that the new theatre has to offer. Corporate Partners membership is available from £5,000 + VAT.

Our current **Corporate Partners** are:

**Bennetts Associates** Architects

SOLOMON TAYLOR & SHAW SOLICITORS

habitat®

We offer a range of other sponsorship opportunities, from performance sponsorship, project support, production sponsorship, education support or even title sponsorship for the entire season. Benefits can be tailored to your needs – please talk to us for more information.

To find out more about any aspect of supporting our work please contact Sarah Coop or Nick Williams in our Development Department on 020 7449 4160 or email development@hampsteadtheatre.com

Hampstead Theatre website sponsored by
DragonNet
*the isp for small business*
dragonnet.co.uk

## Education & Participation Programme

Since its inception in 1998, we have had over 58,000 attendances from aspiring writers and actors aged 5 to 85. Our new home houses a large, dedicated education studio, The Space, which can be transformed from a workshop into a fully equipped performance studio with ease and speed. Local residents and schools are encouraged to make use of the Theatre's expertise and facilities through a number of different projects.

To find out more visit our website, talk to us on 020 7449 4165 or email
education@hampsteadtheatre.com

## Start Nights

A great chance to see the talent of the future flexing its creative muscle.

Start Nights are also an opportunity to present twenty minutes of new material to an audience and gauge their feedback.

Anyone over the age of 16 living, working or studying in Camden, Barnet, Brent or Westminster can participate. Ask at the box office for entry details or check our website.

## Priority Supporters

With advance information and priority booking you can be the first to discover fresh and dynamic playwrights, and make the most of a whole range of discounts for just £12 a year. For more details call us on 020 7722 9301 or email
info@hampsteadtheatre.com

## Cafébar

Open 9.00am to 11.00pm Monday to Saturday, the cafébar offers a generous selection of sandwiches, baguettes, warm paninis, pastas and salads.

You can also order a pre-show supper or an interval snack ahead of time by calling us on 020 7722 9301. Check our website for more information.

Our new building is a stunning venue for celebrations or conferences
for further details email
conferencing@hampsteadtheatre.com or
talk to us on 020 7034 4914.

# hampstead theatre

Anthony Clark **Artistic Director**
James Williams **Executive Director**
Jennie Darnell **Associate Director**
Jeanie O'Hare **Literary Manager**

## Directors
Jenny Abramsky CBE
Jillian Barker
Simon Block
Sir Trevor Chinn CVO
Michael Codron CBE
Lindsay Duncan
Michael Frayn
Tanika Gupta
Amanda Jones
Sir Eddie Kulukundis OBE
Her Honour Judge Angelica Mitchell
Daniel Peltz
Peter Phillips
Paul Rayden
Greg Ripley-Duggan
Patricia Rothman
Vincent Wang (Chairman)

## Administration
Christopher Beard **Finance Manager**
Cath Longman **Administrator**
Joy Aitchison **Finance Officer**
Sajed Chowdry **Administrative Assistant**

## Development
Sarah Coop **Development Director**
Nick Williams **Development Officer**
Helen Hodge **Development Intern**

## Education
Jonathan Siddall **Education Director**
Kelly Wilkinson **Education Associate**
Pippa Ellis **Education & New Writing Co-ordinator**

## Front of House
Victoria Biles **Theatre Manager**
Olivia Wakeford **House Manager**
Lisa Barnes **Front of House Manager**
Jackie Haynes **Head Cleaner**
Thijs Hendriks **Catering Manager**
Martina Wagner **Catering Manager**
**Cleaners:** Almaz Kahsay, Rachael Marks & Sekay Saleh
**Ushers / Box Office Assistants:** Georgina Barnes-Smith, Becky Kitter, Sophie Mosberger & Jacob Tomkins
**Ushers:** David Adcock, Vanessa Airth, Sophia Cable, Emma Campbell-Jones, Geraldine Caulfield, Lynette Cocks, Ann Cross, Joanna Deakin, Claire Duncan, Christopher Hogg, Rachel Holt, Steve Rose & Amy Walker
**Catering Team:** Luis Crespo, Catherine Evans, Christophe Kerhoas, Pia De Keyser, Sally Leonard & Richard Pryal

## Marketing and Box Office
Richard Scandrett **Head of Marketing**
Paul Joyce **Box Office Manager**
Jennifer Rhoads **Marketing Officer**
Christopher Todd **Deputy Box Office Manager**
Hellen Fuller **Box Office Assistant**
Rebecca Kemp **Marketing Assistant**
Colin Knight **Box Office Assistant**

## Production
John Titcombe **Production Manager**
Julie Issott **Company Stage Manager**
Emma Barrow **Assistant Stage Manager**
Greg Gould **Chief Electrician**
Chris Harris **Deputy Electrician**
Simon Williams **Assistant Electrician**
David Tuff **Technical Manager**
Selina Wong **Wardrobe Maintenance**

Hampstead Theatre
Eton Avenue
Swiss Cottage
London
NW3 3EU

info@hampsteadtheatre.com

Box office 020 7722 9301
Textphone 07729 806405
24hr online booking
www.hampsteadtheatre.com

Charity Registration No 218506
Company Registration No 707180
VAT No 230 3818 91

# hampstead theatre

# Autumn Season 2003

**THE STRAITS**
by **Gregory Burke**
29.10.03 – 29.11.03

'THIS SINEWY PRODUCTION IS A WINNER OUT AND OUT, BOASTING TERRIFIC PERFORMANCES FROM ITS YOUNG CAST' THE GUARDIAN

**METEORITE**
by **Barbara Norden**
04.12.03 – 03.01.04

**REVELATIONS**
by **Stephen Lowe**
10.12.03 – 31.01.04

A gloriously comic exploration of the age old confusions between love and sexual desire.

**THE STRAITS**

'A SPLENDID NEW HOME FOR NEW WRITING'
DAILY TELEGRAPH

650 tickets per week available @ £6.50
for under 26s and people on full benefit.

**Box office** 020 7722 9301    **Online booking** www.hampsteadtheatre.com

## DONMAR

Six London friends, whose lives and work are overshadowed by a demanding film producer, flee the country for a weekend to escape his clutches.

Safely ensconced in a hotel in Amsterdam, the uneasy equilibrium that has existed between them is joyously exposed as the alcohol starts to flow.

**11 SEPTEMBER - 15 NOVEMBER 2003**

# The Hotel in Amsterdam
### by John Osborne

**Cast**
ALEX BECKETT
ADRIAN BOWER
ANTHONY CALF
SELINA GRIFFITHS
SUSANNAH HARKER
TOM HOLLANDER
LAURA HOWARD
DARRI INGOLFSSON
OLIVIA WILLIAMS

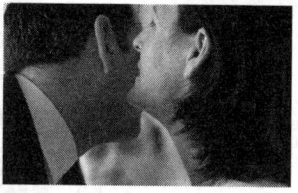

**Director**
ROBIN LEFEVRE
**Designer**
LIZ ASCROFT
**Lighting Designer**
MICK HUGHES

PRINCIPAL SPONSOR
THE BEST-RUN BUSINESSES RUN SAP — **SAP**

---

20 November 2003 - 7 February 2004

## After Miss Julie
A version of Strindberg's *Miss Julie* by Patrick Marber
Michael Grandage directs Helen Baxendale, Richard Coyle & Kelly Reilly

**BOX OFFICE 0870 060 6624**
NO BOOKING FEE

***ticketmaster*** **0870 160 2878**
CC 24 HOUR BOOKING FEE

www.donmarwarehouse.com

---

## Tricycle — 269 Kilburn High Road NW6

11 September - 25 October
The Tricycle Theatre presents the 100th anniversary (well nearly!) of

# John Bull's Other Island
## By Bernard Shaw
Directed by Dominic Dromgoole

Written in 1904 with a satirical wit that makes it feel like yesterday, this hilarious comedy tears into the national identities of the English and Irish, and spares no-one.

> **"Unspeakably delightful"**
> Rupert Brook

**Box Office 020 7328 1000   www.tricycle.co.uk**

# ᴛʜᴇREP
Birmingham Repertory Theatre

Birmingham Repertory Theatre is one of Britain's leading national theatre companies. From its base in Birmingham, The REP produces over twenty new productions each year. This Spring, critics praised Jonathan Church and Rachel Kavanaugh's production of David Hare's trilogy of plays (**Racing Demon, Murmuring Judges** & **The Absence of War**) first seen at the National Theatre 10 years ago and never since performed in their entirety anywhere in the UK.

In 1998 the company launched The Door, a venue dedicated to the production and presentation of new work. Through the extensive commissioning of new work The REP is providing vital opportunities for the young and emerging writing talent that will lead the way in the theatre of the future.

The theatre's Autumn-Winter 2003 season has seen new productions of Arthur Miller's **A View From The Bridge** and Alan Bennett's **The Madness of George III**, and this Christmas we will be producing the legendary musical **The Wizard of Oz**.

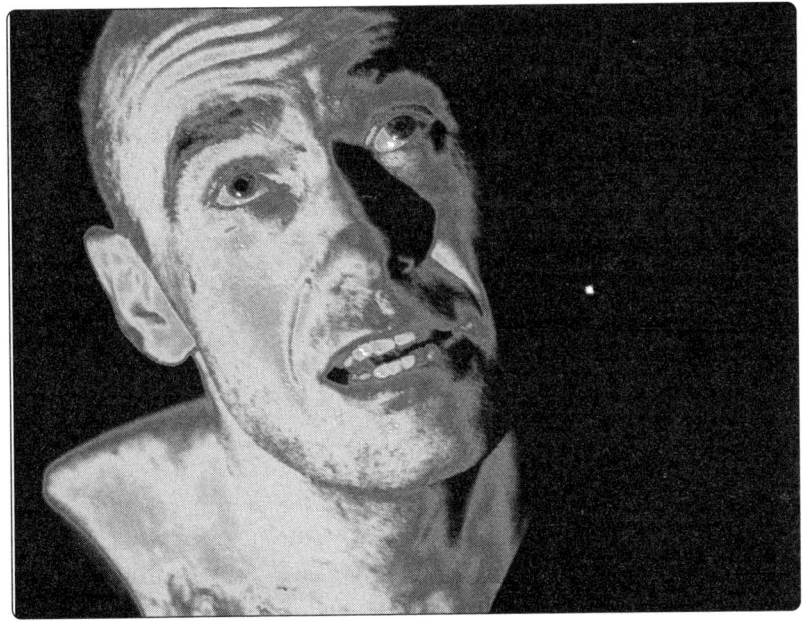

REP productions regularly transfer to London and tour nationally and internationally. Our acclaimed production of Steinbeck's **Of Mice And Men** embarked on a major UK tour in February and can currently be seen in the West End, and our production of **Hamlet**, co-produced with this year's Edinburgh International Festival toured to Dublin and Barcelona. Previous productions that have been seen in London in recent years include **The Snowman, Two Pianos, Four Hands, Baby Doll, My Best Friend, Terracotta, The Gift, A Wedding Story, Out In The Open, Tender, Behsharam** and **The Ramayana.**

Artistic Director Jonathan Church
Executive Director Stuart Rogers
Associate Director (Literary) Ben Payne

www.birmingham-rep.co.uk
Box Office 0121 236 4455

# The Door

The production of work by living writers has always been central to the work of the company since it was founded by Sir Barry Jackson in 1913. The Door was established in 1998 in The REP's old studio space, as a theatre dedicated to the production and presentation of new plays.

The company develops and commissions work from the most exciting writers from both the region and beyond. Our aim is to create a year-round season of diverse, contemporary work that combines our own productions with presentations of the most interesting plays touring the country.

The Door supports the development of young writers, performers and directors – particularly through Transmissions, our young writers' programme which culminates each year in a very lively summer festival.

The Door also provides a home for new ideas, artists and companies. The REP pioneered the Attachment Programme for writers; a scheme which enables new and established writers to explore a new idea for a play in tandem with a professional producing company. Many of the plays seen in The Door began life in this way and have gone on to be co-produced and seen in theatres all over the country and abroad. In 2003/2004 we will embark on a unique scheme to support the development of new plays for very young audiences, funded by Arts Council England.

For more information on the Attachment Programme and our future plans for The Door, please contact Ben Payne or Caroline Jester in the Literary Department at The REP on 0121 245 2000.

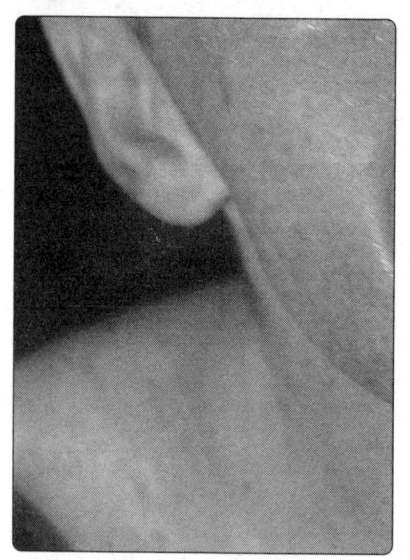

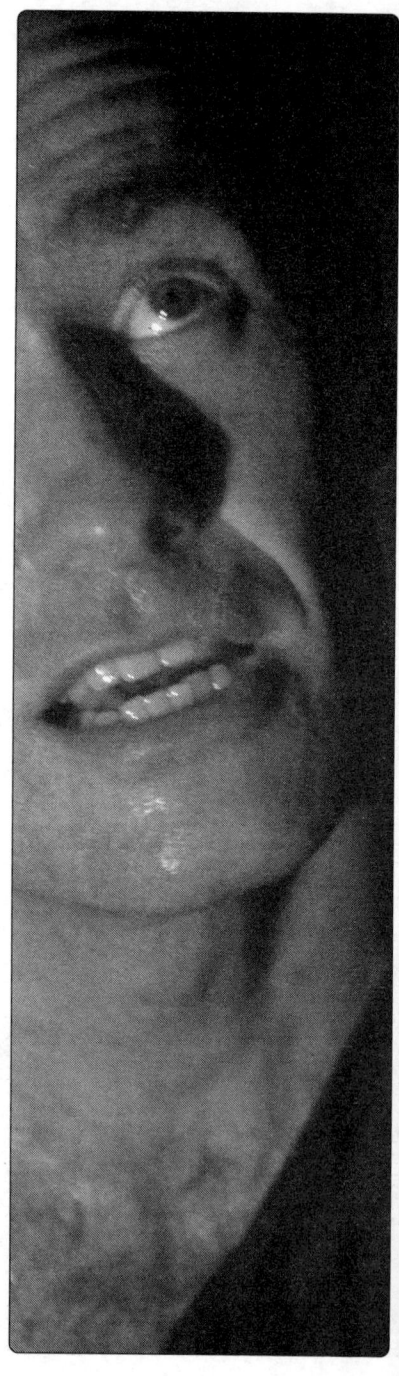

# Transmissions

Transmissions is The REP's unique project aimed at nurturing the playwrights of the future. It gives twenty young people from across the West Midlands region the chance to develop their writing skills in a constructive and creative way.

Transmissions writers are given the opportunity of working with professional playwrights Carl Miller and Noël Greig to develop initial ideas into full and complete scripts through a series of workshops.

The scheme allows participants to meet other writers in a fun and interactive environment, giving them the support and encouragement needed to expand their interest into an active process with a very definite aim; to see their work performed on stage by professional actors.

In June each year the writers come together with professional directors, actors and designers to present a showcase of their work in Transmissions Festival. The festival is a celebration of their work, enabling them to gain an insight into the collaborative process involved in theatre once the initial writing stage is complete.

Photo Credit Robert Day

This year's Transmissions Festival was another runaway success and the scheme has now helped to develop the work of over one hundred young writers.

'Transmissions hurtled into its second week, blazing with energy and delivering some of the most provocative and original new work to be seen anywhere in the city'. Birmingham Post

'A rich and extraordinary assortment of tomorrow's talent' Evening Mail

'It is a brilliant enterprise' Birmingham Post

If you would like to become involved with Transmissions or want further information about the festival please contact Caroline Jester in the Literary Department at The REP on 0121 245 2000.

# THE MATHS TUTOR

Clare McIntyre

**Characters**

ANNA

TOM

J.J.

PAUL

JANE

BRIAN

*A double slash // means that the next character to speak starts speaking at that point.*

# PART ONE

## Scene One

ANNA *lets herself into 'Heather Cottage'. She comes in through the back door which opens straight into the kitchen. A holiday cottage. Basic stuff. Rudimentary furnishings. Hasn't been touched, altered in years. The sort of place which is fine in the summer because you spend most of your time outside but on the spartan side and uninviting at any other time. It is a bright and sunny day during the Half Term holiday. That said; it's not exactly hot.*

ANNA *has a holdall with her and a carrier bag. She puts the holdall down and puts the carrier bag on the kitchen table with the keys to the cottage. She looks about her, taking the place in. She is unimpressed. She sits down and looks at her watch. She takes two bottles of wine out of the carrier bag. She takes out her mobile and punches in a number. She gets an answerphone.*

ANNA. Jeremy darling it's me. Phone me. Please. I'm going to die here. It's like a bloody youth hostel. When did you last see 'Formica'? (*She chuckles.*) And 'Fablon'? You don't even know what Fablon is do you? Way before your time. It's nasty old plastic covering stuff: the sort of thing my Granny had on all her shelves. You didn't miss anything! The place has got a charm I suppose. I don't know how I'd pitch it though. 'Room proportions are excellent. Double aspect kitchen.' Roomy certainly. 'Original features' I suppose. I haven't had a look yet. 'Original seaside English' . . . Phone me darling. Love you. Kiss kiss.

*She puts her phone in her pocket and has a look for a cork screw. She finds one and opens one of the bottles of wine. She pours herself a glass.*

*Blackout.*

## Scene Two

TOM *is marking out a goal on the beach not far from 'Heather Cottage'. J.J. is sitting on the ball staring into space while* TOM *marks out a goal in the sand.*

TOM. That okay?

    J.J. *doesn't answer.*

    J.J. (*Beat.*) That okay?

    *Again* J.J. *doesn't answer.*

    (*Louder.*) J.J.

J.J. (*turning round*). What?

TOM. Why are you wearing shades? The sun went in ages ago.

J.J. I'm having a black mood day.

TOM. What's the matter?

J.J. I wish I was a dog.

TOM. What?

J.J. Look at that daft bloody dog. All it needs is a plastic picnic bottle blowing along the beach.

    TOM *kicks the ball out from under* J.J.

TOM. I think dogs are boring.

    *He dribbles niftily round* J.J. *who still doesn't respond.*

    Come on!

    TOM *manoeuvres himself past* J.J. *and shoots straight into the goal.* J.J. *doesn't pay any attention.* TOM *picks up the ball and comes over to* J.J.

    What's the matter?

J.J. Would your Mum tell you something?

TOM. What do you mean?

J.J. If there was something she should tell you would she tell you?

TOM. You mean like something that was going to affect me? Like them going to separate? Or something happening to Alice?

J.J. No. Not sisters I haven't got a sister. Something really important.

TOM. Alice is important.

J.J. Why? She's only your sister.

TOM. It's something you can't know J.J.

J.J. Yeah. Well. Whatever. Would she?

TOM. What?

J.J. Would she hold something back from you?

TOM. Who? Alice?

J.J. No. Your Mum.

TOM. What?

J.J. A secret she should tell you.

TOM. What sort of secret?

J.J. I don't know. Just a secret.

TOM. Suppose it would depend.

J.J. On what?

TOM. On why it was a secret.

J.J. Something she should tell you that she knows she should tell you. Would she tell you?

TOM. That's a secret?

J.J. Yeah.

TOM. It would depend why it was a secret.

J.J. Fuck's sake. BE . . . CAUSE!

TOM *goes back to dribbling with the ball.*

Would she Tom? Keep something from you?

TOM. I don't know.

J.J. Something really, really important.

TOM. Like what?

J.J. That's the point. I can't tell you what. Something mega.

TOM. People don't tell secrets. That's why they're secrets.

J.J. Even when they should. Listen will you.

TOM *stops.*

TOM. If they tell you they're not proper secrets are they?

J.J. But would she tell you something she should tell you?

TOM. I suppose so.

J.J. Thought so. (*Beat.*) Parents are shit.

TOM. What's happened?

J.J. Complete crap. Total, fuckin' pile a' shit.

TOM. J.J.?

J.J. Nothing.

J.J. *gets up and starts to play. They kick the ball about together.* TOM *goes in goal and* J.J. *shoots.*

Fuck parents.

TOM. Do you want to go back?

J.J. No.

TOM. What's the matter?

J.J. My Mum's disgusting. She's got a new boyfriend. He's horrible. Hideous. I hate him. Bastard.

*He kicks the ball hard.* TOM *misses it and has to go after it.*

TOM. Don't take it out on me.

J.J. *sits back down.* TOM *joins him with the ball.*

Why don't you like him?

J.J. He doesn't like me.

TOM. How do you know?

J.J. He's got hairy arms. He's got really, really hairy arms. He's a fucking gorilla. She's fucking a fucking gorilla.

TOM. How long's she known him?

J.J. Feels like for ever.

TOM. Do his laugh. You're good at laughs.

J.J. He never bloody laughs.

TOM. He must do.

J.J. He's never laughed at anything I've ever said.

TOM. Maybe he doesn't find you funny.

J.J. He doesn't find me anything but a fucking nuisance. He's never had a fucking conversation with me. He's never ever talked to me about anything. Ever.

TOM (*laughing*). So he's a gorilla who doesn't speak.

J.J. (*starting to do an impression*). He's got a really, really silly little high voice. 'How's tricks J.J.?' He makes me sick. He's there every fucking weekend. 'How's it going J.J.? How's it going?' He's like a bloody parrot.

TOM. At least he speaks to you.

J.J. Big deal. That's what you say to someone when you don't know what to say. He doesn't want to know.

TOM. Maybe he's . . . I don't know. Maybe he's trying.

J.J. He's not interested. And mum gets all cuddly and sweet with him. It's disgusting.

TOM. Why?

J.J. Deep throat bollocks in front of me.

TOM (*stands up*). Come on. Let's play.

J.J. (*stands*). Jane and Paul don't do that do they?

TOM *resumes kicking the ball about a bit.*

TOM. Nope.

J.J. *joins in.*

J.J. Mum says they're in love.

TOM. You'd better start liking him then.

J.J. Yuk.

J.J. *hits the ball wide and goes off to retrieve it.*

TOM. You wanker.

J.J. Wanker yourself.

TOM. Do you do lots of sport?

J.J. Every day.

TOM. Every day!

J.J. Yeah.

TOM. Posh school.

J.J. Don't you?

TOM. No. We haven't even got our own pitch.

J.J. Poor school.

TOM. It's not poor. It's just not posh.

J.J. You know your parents –

TOM. They're the parents I've got.

J.J. At least you've got yours.

TOM. You've got yours.

J.J. They're not together, though.

## Scene Three

*The kitchen at 'Heather Cottage'. It is empty. The partially-drunk bottle of wine and* ANNA*'s glass are on the table.*

JANE (*off stage*). You can do that later. Sort your room out first.

  PAUL *comes in laden down with beach stuff – towels, lilo, wet suits. He plonks the things down, sees the wine on the table and calls:*

PAUL. Anna?

  JANE *comes in with the rest of the beach stuff: plastic bags, picnic basket etc.*

JANE. Where is she? (*Calls.*) Anna?

PAUL. Maybe she's gone for a walk.

  ANNA *comes through the other door into the room.*

ANNA. No. I'm here. I was just having a snooze. Hi. Isn't this place absolutely fabulous?

PAUL. You got here?

ANNA. No probs at all. Hello Jane.

JANE. Hello Anna. You've finally made it to 'Heather Cottage'.

ANNA. It's gorgeous.

JANE. We actually bought it when I was pregnant with Tom. Paul's mother was going to put some money in trust for Alice and Tom but we persuaded her to put it into the cottage instead. Strictly speaking it's not even ours.

PAUL. Now you know what we've been going on about for the last . . .

ANNA. If I'd known about it in the beginning, well, I'd've gazumped you myself. No, but joking aside, people would kill to have a bolt hole like this.

> J.J. *and* TOM *come in from outside. They go straight through the room and exit through the other door going into the house. On his way* TOM *says:*

TOM. Hello Anna.

ANNA. Hello Tom.

> *The boys exit towards the bedrooms upstairs.*

'Hello Mum. Good journey?' 'Fine thank you darling.' (*Beat.*) Why isn't J.J. a delightfully courteous boy like Tom?

PAUL. He's been grand.

ANNA. Honestly?

JANE. No trouble at all.

PAUL. Mind: we've got it cracked.

ANNA. How do you mean?

PAUL. We keep them very tired. Very tired. It's non stop from the moment they get up. Get the drift wood. Clean out the fire. Lay a new fire. French cricket in the garden. Football on the beach. Into their bathing costumes. Into the sea.

ANNA. But it's freezing!

JANE. Not to Paul. He turns into a fitness freak when he's here.

PAUL. Crawl across. Breaststroke back.

JANE. He's had them thrashing over the bay every day. Then he has them running round the beach to dry off. They're got to go right round and it's a big beach.

PAUL. We've got them on the go from dawn till dusk.

ANNA (*laughing*). Would you like to have J.J. seven days a week?

PAUL. He really has been great.

JANE. And it's wonderful for Tom to have him with us. He's not having to spend his half-term with the 'old folks'.

ANNA. I'd hardly call you two 'old folks'.

PAUL. Thank you Anna. (*To* JANE.) You speak for yourself.

JANE. I'd better go and hang these things up while the weather's fine.

ANNA. The boys should do that.

JANE. No. They've got plenty to do.

ANNA. Can I help?

JANE. No. You sit and relax.

ANNA. Really?

JANE. Absolutely. I won't be a moment.

PAUL. Can you manage darling?

JANE. 'Course I can.

*JANE gathers the wet suits and takes them outside.*

ANNA. I feel terribly spoilt.

PAUL. Not a bit of it. You're our guest.

ANNA. What on earth are they for?

PAUL. The wet suits?

ANNA. Is that what they are?

PAUL. You're not much of an outdoors girl.

ANNA. God no.

PAUL. They're for windsurfing. Once they've had a swim and a run so they've dried off a bit, they get into their wet suits for a bit of windsurfing. They need them if they're going to stay in the water. We're not talking Mediterranean here!

ANNA. J.J.'s been having the time of his life!

PAUL That's what this place is for. J.J.'s been using Alice's old suit.

ANNA. Oh right. Of course. Does Alice still come down here herself?

PAUL. She's not much into family holidays these days. (*Referring to the wine bottle.*) May I?

ANNA. Yes. Of course.

PAUL *pours a couple of glasses of wine.*

PAUL. Thank you. This is very good of you.

ANNA. I never travel without.

PAUL. The perfect guest. Have you parked your bag somewhere?

ANNA. Yes. I've put myself upstairs. I don't know if . . .

PAUL. That's fine. Jane'll sort it out in a bit.

J.J. *hurries on.*

ANNA. Er . . . 'Hello'? 'Hello Mummy'? (*Beat.*) Come here. Let Mummy give you a kiss.

J.J. *goes to her and she puts her arms round him and gives him a kiss.*

That's better. Having a good time?

J.J. Yeah. Great. Tom wants to know how much we should take.

PAUL. What you need.

J.J. Okay.

*He starts to go.*

ANNA. What are you doing?

J.J. We're sorting our stuff out.

ANNA. Oh. Right. Off you go then.

J.J. *exits towards the bedrooms.*

'Don't let me interfere. I'm only your mother.' I suppose he does see me every day of the week, 365 days of the year but still.

PAUL (*drinking his wine*). This wine's very nice.

ANNA. It's 'don't speak to mother' time. Don't even acknowledge her. She's only there to pay the bills.

PAUL. He's been grand.

ANNA. Now he's being fifteen.

PAUL. That's what they're like.

ANNA. I blame testosterone.

PAUL. We poor boys.

ANNA. It still gets on my nerves.

PAUL. He's very excited.

ANNA. I know. I know. I know. I'm a hard mother.

PAUL. Of course you are.

ANNA. Unfortunately I am. Joking aside. I'm always so bloody tired.

PAUL. How is work?

ANNA. The demands are absurd. It's never ending. I've recently 'completed', that magic word, with clients who were never available to view property, who moaned all the time about the details of properties they were sent, who moaned more about the things they did go and see, and who moaned with each other whenever they came into the office and found me, who was their favourite target to have a joint moan at. They were 'The moaners'. And now they owe us money and they'll be moaning with each other about having to pay it. It's delightful. I love every single minute of it.

PAUL. Are they typical?

ANNA. You get all sorts. It's fine really. The plus is it's a good job. The minus is the hours.

PAUL. And having to deal with horrible people?

ANNA. Don't you have that problem?

PAUL. Thankfully not at the moment. Provided I've got a good team round me I enjoy it.

ANNA. But you work in a pretty difficult area?

PAUL. Being with a charity you mean?

ANNA. It must be distressing.

PAUL. It is. Of course. People's lives are hell. But I leave at five. And we do good work.

ANNA. That's the plus.

PAUL. That's the plus. Both Jane and I are nine to fivers I'm afraid. It's in the nature. Dull I suppose but . . . us. And good for Tom 'cos Jane's only part-time receptionist at the practice. But we do have excellent teeth! Dull jobs have their perks.

JANE *comes in.*

All done?

JANE. Yup.

ANNA. Can I pour you a glass?

JANE. Thank you.

ANNA *pours* JANE *a glass of wine.*

ANNA. It's a funny thing you know but sometimes J.J. can be such a handful I forget our single sex, single parent household isn't necessarily the norm.

PAUL. There's lots of family history in this little cottage.

ANNA. How wonderful.

JANE. It's seen the ups and downs.

PAUL. Not many downs.

JANE. No. True. (*Beat.*) Actually there've only been weather downs.

ANNA. Well it's England.

PAUL. And the odd bit of illness.

JANE. When have we had anybody ill here?

PAUL. Tom. (*Beat.*) When he was five.

JANE. I don't remember.

PAUL. You must do. You spent weeks here with him when he had mumps.

JANE. Of course.

PAUL. Jane was marvellous. She kept him occupied the whole time. Poor little soul was miserable.

JANE. Wasn't he?

PAUL. Do you still have that wonderful costume you made for him?

JANE. The badger costume?

PAUL. Yes. It was great.

JANE. Probably. I never throw anything away. It'll still be in the dressing-up box.

PAUL. Why don't you go and have a look?

JANE. Shall I?

PAUL. I'd love to see it again. I remember it being tremendous.

JANE. Okay.

*She goes off to look for the costume.*

ANNA. The two of you are amazing.

PAUL. Why?

ANNA. You both love it don't you?

PAUL. What?

ANNA. Being parents.

PAUL. Don't all parents?

ANNA. Of course.

PAUL. They're everything. Our children. To us.

ANNA. The two of you have so much energy.

PAUL. Do you think?

ANNA. Fantastic.

PAUL. Thank you.

ANNA. Tom's very lucky. J.J. could do with a male influence. I could! It's hard being a single parent.

PAUL. I'm sure. I just delight in still having Tom. I can play to my heart's content.

ANNA. And very macho games it sounds like.

PAUL. Keeps you fit.

ANNA. And young.

PAUL. Most important of all.

ANNA. No wonder you get down here as often as you do.

PAUL. To get my fix, supping at the fountain of eternal youth.

ANNA. You do look very good for your age.

PAUL. Thank you.

ANNA. Has he been eating you out of house and home?

PAUL. I think I've got the biggest appetite. We all eat Jane out of house and home.

*He hears the boys coming. They come on with loads of bedding – duvets, pillows, blankets.*

Don't we?

J.J. What?

PAUL. Have good appetites here. (*He sees how much they have brought in.*) Have you left anything for Anna?

TOM. Mum's going to do that.

ANNA. For me?

PAUL. We're putting you upstairs and the boys are going to be in the tent.

ANNA (*to* TOM). Is that okay?

TOM. Yeah. It's cool.

ANNA. You won't sleep a wink. You'll talk all night.

PART ONE    17

J.J. We won't.

ANNA. No?

J.J. We're going to have the telly.

PAUL. You might have the telly if I can get it together.

J.J. You promised.

ANNA. J.J.

J.J. What?

PAUL. One thing at a time. Leave this stuff here. Get the tent up first. Come back when you've done that and we'll see what we can do about the telly.

*The boys put the bedding down and go outside.*

Okay?

TOM. Fine.

ANNA. Is this alright?

PAUL. Of course it is. They'll have a wonderful time.

ANNA. They certainly will if they can watch telly all night.

PAUL. We'll have to get to the shops before they shut because we'll need an extension lead.

ANNA. I'll pay for that.

PAUL. Don't be silly. It's only a few quid.

ANNA. It's J.J.'s idea I bet.

PAUL. I think it was actually.

ANNA. 'Big Brother.' Can't be missed.

*JANE comes on. She is wearing the 'badger' costume over her clothes. She has a pair of black gloves with false nails attached which are painted black and an animal nose from a joke shop. And a head-dress come cape which is attached to her head: a very home-made affair of black material with bits of fake fur attached. From the back you can see what she was trying to achieve: there is a strip of grey white from the crown of her head down her back to her waist. It's held in place with a tie round her middle. She parades.*

JANE. There!

PAUL (*laughing*). Isn't that priceless?

JANE. It's good isn't it?

ANNA. I'm impressed. Terribly. I don't remember making that much effort for J.J. Not when he had mumps. I don't remember him having mumps.

JANE. It was special because he had it here. We made it together.

PAUL (*calls*). Tom. J.J.

JANE. A spectacular creation you have to admit.

PAUL (*laughing*). It's wonderful! Wonderful. You look completely and utterly barmy.

JANE. I think I must be. I remember taking hours making it.

ANNA. I can see.

JANE. It's my 'not quite a badger' costume.

ANNA. Oh.

*She shows off the back.*

JANE. See?

ANNA. Oh yes.

PAUL. Hilarious! (*Beat.*) Where are those boys? They've got to see this. (*Calls.*) Tom! J.J.! Come and see Jane.

ANNA. Amazing you've still got it.

JANE. I'm a bit sentimental. There's a box of stuff up there from his childhood. And Alice's. I think you've got to have dressing-up things for children. This has done sterling service over the years.

PAUL. My wife isn't shy. Vanity has no place in her makeup. If it's in a good cause she'll go the whole hog.

JANE. There are loads of badgers round here but we never saw one. So we got creative.

PAUL. It certainly is a creation. An 'A' for effort. Not remotely like a badger in any way. It's a homemade job in a . . .

JANE (*interrupts*). It is.

PAUL. Darling. Badgers are sleek, agile, nocturnal burrowers.

JANE. I should have had a torch!

PAUL. No. You're a sedentary sort of badger. Not the lithe and athletic member of the set. A bit of a stay-at-home bulky sort of badger. An embarrassment to the set.

JANE. You're so mean!

PAUL. It's a bit of a passion killer darling. You're a lumpy badger. That's it: lumpy. I'm going to call you 'Lumpy'.

*The boys come on.*

What do you think of 'Lumpy'?

*The boys laugh.* PAUL *and* JANE *do as well.* ANNA *doesn't find it funny.*

JANE. 'Not quite a badger'.

TOM. What?

JANE. That's what you said when you saw it. It's my 'not quite a badger' costume. Do you remember it? (TOM *looks doubtful.*) I made it for you when you were little. And that was your verdict.

TOM. I was mean. It's good.

PAUL. Mrs Lumpy.

J.J. Can we do the telly now?

ANNA. J.J. wait until . . .

PAUL. No we need to go and sort that out. J.J.'s right.

J.J. I've got the money.

PAUL. What money?

J.J. For the extension lead.

PAUL. Don't worry about that.

J.J. I've got twenty quid.

ANNA. Since when?

J.J. I have.

ANNA. You didn't have any when I spoke to you.

J.J. I've got it now.

ANNA. You do not go through my purse without speaking to me.

J.J. Can we go and get it?

ANNA. Listen to me.

J.J. Yeah. Yeah. Yeah.

ANNA. Don't talk to me like that.

J.J. Can we?

ANNA. When did you go through my purse?

J.J. It was upstairs.

ANNA. You're very naughty J.J.

J.J. We need it.

ANNA. That's not the point. You know you do not go through my purse without asking me.

J.J. Yeah. Yeah. Yeah.

ANNA. I mean it.

*Pause.*

PAUL. We'll get off and do it now.

TOM. What about the tent?

PAUL. We'll do that when we get back. You can bring the bedding out now though.

*The boys go towards the door.*

You and Anna can talk in peace.

JANE (*leaving*). I'll get out of this.

*Blackout.*

## Scene Four

*Later on the same day. J.J. and TOM are on a vantage point on a cliff top walk near Heather Cottage. They are sharing an expensive-looking pair of binoculars and looking out to sea.*

J.J. I hope he can fix the reception.

TOM. He will. It's best to stay out of the way.

J.J. It's a new series.

TOM. I know.

J.J. The tent won't leak, will it?

TOM. Of course not.

J.J. Because if it rains, we could get electrocuted.

TOM. It's not going to rain. It's a beautiful evening.

*Beat.*

J.J. Will they watch it?

TOM. The sunset?

J.J. Big Brother.

TOM. Who? Mum and Dad?

J.J. My Mum's glued to it.

TOM. Mum won't. Dad'll have a look when she's not there.

*Beat.*

J.J. What did your Dad say they were called?

TOM. What?

J.J. Those seals we should look out for.

TOM. Halichoerus grypus.

J.J. What kind of a name is that?

TOM. A Latin one.

J.J. In English.

TOM. Hooked-nose pig of the sea.

*Beat.*

J.J. Don't see the point of Latin. No one speaks it.

TOM. Gardeners use it.

J.J. It's dead.

TOM. Plants have Latin names.

J.J. Are you saying gardeners talk Latin?

TOM. No thicko.

J.J. Don't fucking call me that.

TOM. Joke.

J.J. My mum's always saying I'm stupid.

TOM. Sorry. See that jackdaw's nest about two-thirds of the way up the cliff on the right?

J.J. Have you ever done it with a girl? // I can't see anything.

TOM. Might have.

*He gives the glasses to* J.J.

J.J. Where? // I mean like all the way?

TOM. You see the tree on its own near the edge of the headland. Right? OK. Now go to the gorse bush –

J.J. The what?

TOM. The gorse bush.

J.J. Where?

TOM. This way. The bush with the bright yellow flowers. Got it.

J.J. OK.

TOM. So get the top of the cliff about half way in but slightly nearer the tree and go down.

J.J. Can't see a thing. (*He hands the binoculars back.*)

*Beat.*

I had this girlfriend called Monica and I told Mum we were sleeping together. She was cool about it and let us do it at home as long as we were safe and stuff.

TOM. Lucky you.

J.J. She boasts about it to her friends.

TOM. How old's Monica?

J.J. Was fifteen.

TOM (*gives up looking*). Maybe it's not a jackdaw.

J.J. Did your Dad do Latin at school?

TOM. I think so. But he learnt the name of those seals from an old encyclopedia we have in the cottage. He was 'rainy-day-afternoon-browsing'.

J.J. He knows some really weird stuff your dad does.

TOM. He calls it fishing for facts in peculiar rivers.

J.J. You what?

TOM. It's a quote. He likes quotes. Remember that stuff about oracular proof.

J.J. Well weird.

TOM. And you think your Mum's weird.

J.J. Yeah but she can't help it. She's an estate agent.

*Beat.*

Let's have another look?

TOM *hands him the binoculars again.*

There's a dog down there swimming. I think it might be that one we saw before.

TOM. Shouldn't think so. Loads of people have dogs round here.

J.J. (*putting the binoculars down*). You do lots of things with your Dad don't you?

TOM. Suppose.

J.J. Does he ask what you're going to be when you grow up?

TOM. What?

J.J. Jeremy's always asking me that? What are you going to be when you grow up J.J.?

TOM. I want to learn Spanish and play for Real Madrid.

J.J. In your dreams.

*Beat.*

TOM. So what do you say to him?

J.J. Fuck off Hairy. What's it to you?

TOM. You don't.

J.J. I wish. I say mind your own business you're not my Dad and Mum says don't be so rude. He's only taking an interest. She asked me once and I told her I was going to leave school and do stuff with computers and be a billionaire by the time I'm twenty. And Mum says 'Darling that's a good idea but you'll need some qualifications.' She's so annoying sometimes.

TOM. Is that why your Mum's making you do extra maths?

J.J. That's what she pretends but actually she's just copying your Mum. Your Mum told her she was fixing extra lessons for you so she thought it would look good if she did it. Like she really cares or something. I asked her if I could have my own computer if I passed.

TOM. What did she say?

J.J. She said I'm not getting into bribes J.J. (*Peers through the binoculars again.*)

*Beat.*

My teachers keep telling her I won't pass anyway. That I could do well if I wasn't so lazy. I could do well if they were any good.

TOM. I'm no good at maths but Mum and Dad say I must pass it to keep my options open. I've got to pass maths to go to a proper university, like Alice. That's why they arranged Brian. Brian's a better teacher than the one we've got at school.

J.J. For you maybe.

TOM. Anyway, we've been let off for a week.

J.J. We've still got to do homework though.

*Beat.*

I think I can see one

TOM. What? A seal? Where?

J.J. Right out there. Where that round rock is, where the beach curves round on the left.

TOM. It's more likely to be a harbour seal than a halichoerus grypus. You can't really tell from here. It's getting dark. Could be a piece of driftwood. We'd better get back. I'm starving.

J.J. I hope the telly's working.

TOM. If it isn't we can play chess.

J.J. Or backgammon. I'm good at backgammon.

*Blackout.*


### Scene Five

*Some time later.* ANNA *and* JANE *are sitting on chairs outside Heather Cottage. They have their glasses of wine.*

ANNA (*laughing*). I used to stop myself. Get nearly there. On the verge of being there. Almost enjoying myself. Nearly

letting go. Nearly actually getting there. But I didn't.
I wouldn't. I burst into tears instead. Quietly. Unobtrusively.
You know: just the wet down the side of your face crying.
Un-bloody-believable really. Can't recognise myself when
I think about it now. Me! Bloody insane. Me not managing
to come? Not believable. Not credible. Not possible. Bloody
Hell. I make damned sure I do come. (*Beat.*) I'm shocking
you. Sorry.

JANE. You're not.

ANNA. I can't remember how I got onto it.

JANE. I asked you . . .

ANNA. Of course: Tom. Growing up and all the pains.

JANE. I just asked // what you

ANNA (*interrupts*). How you introduce the little darlings to sex.

JANE. Not quite as . . .

ANNA. And I blathered on straight away about myself. Typical.

JANE. I'm . . . er . . . I'm not as . . .

ANNA. Big mouth just got straight in.

JANE. It's alright.

ANNA. I shouldn't have done that.

JANE. I don't mind.

ANNA. I'm a terrible one for talking about myself. And I'm sure you don't want to hear about my early dramas discovering sex.

JANE. I'm not as . . .

ANNA. You don't talk about it that readily.

JANE. I don't know that you need to. Alice got through growing up without any pain; no disasters.

ANNA. But you're worried about Tom?

JANE. I'm not worried.

ANNA. 'Cos I'll talk to him if you like. I'm good at that.

JANE. No. No I don't want that at all.

ANNA. I'm a very up-front person with all this. You've got to be with young people nowadays. It's your duty. You have to be.

JANE. I don't know I agree.

ANNA. Of course you have.

JANE. Why?

ANNA. Because of the way things are now.

JANE. Nothing's taboo.

ANNA. Absolutely. (*Beat.*) But it's not like it was for us. It's not the Fab sixties and whatever-they-were seventies. (*Beat.*) That's why I was talking about me. That's what set me off. It was alright to be an ignorant . . . In fact it wasn't alright to be ignorant at all. It wasn't. It's never alright to be ignorant. But the dangers were different. That's what I was trying to say.

JANE. I see.

ANNA. I mean you know: what was the worst thing that could happen to us?

*Pause.*

JANE. I don't know. You could fall for the wrong man?

ANNA. And what could happen?

JANE. You'd be unhappy. (*Beat.*) I'm bit out of my depth: I only had a couple of boyfriends before Paul.

ANNA. You could get pregnant. (*Beat.*) That would have been your fear wouldn't it? (*Beat.*) It certainly was mine. We all grow up for God's sake. We're going to make mistakes. It's probably why I'm fanatical about it now. It's so important to get it right.

JANE. Yes.

ANNA. Isn't it?

JANE. What?

ANNA. How we introduce them to sex.

JANE. Oh.

ANNA. It's vital.

JANE. You leave it to nature; you've got to.

ANNA. What? Now?

JANE. Why not? They're going to // find out

ANNA (*interrupts*). It's all changed. It's a different thing now.

JANE. Why?

ANNA. Because it's dangerous now. It's deadly seriously dangerous now. It's not just about falling pregnant by mistake it could be about dying for heaven's sake. That's how it's different. (*Beat.*) I made damned sure J.J. got off to the right start.

JANE. J.J.?

ANNA. Oh yes. Darling little J.J.'s at it already. He's got a girlfriend called Monica. Or he did have. She might just have been a first experience thing. I don't know. He doesn't talk about her so . . . But he's done it. He's got it over with. And I made sure he did it safely. Up the stairs he went with the condoms in his hand.

JANE. He's a child.

ANNA. Don't you believe it. Fifteen's standard nowadays.

JANE. Sometimes. I want Tom to have as much childhood as he can.

ANNA. We all do but you can't stop them.

JANE. I think he's got a bit of time to go yet.

ANNA. You can never be too sure.

JANE. He hasn't shown any signs of anything yet.

ANNA. They're secretive little things.

JANE. I'm sure he'd talk to me if he wanted to. Alice did.

ANNA. I wouldn't bank on it. You don't know what's going on in their little heads. Any of them. Even J.J. And I'm an up-front person when it comes to sex. He's always known Mummy has boyfriends. Since the divorce that is which is five years ago now. Of course it's different for you: you don't have that problem.

JANE. No.

ANNA. Well I've had several relationships since then. Good. Bad. You name it. So J.J. is used to Mummy having . . . well . . . having a sex life. It isn't all about sex obviously. I'm not perverse. I'm normal. (*Laughs.*) What's normal for heaven's sake. I'm a normal woman. I need a sex life. I didn't want him growing up with me not having a life. That isn't normal is it? Just because I'd left his father didn't mean I was just his Mummy. (*Beat.*) It's the big one Jane. It really is. Oh boy is it when you're on your own. I had to decide there and then how I was going to do it, how I was going to have my life and his life, how we were going to do the thing together. It's a choice. You either decide you're going to have an adult life which I knew I absolutely had to have or not. I knew I had to make it absolutely clear from the start that he was going to have to get used to me having a private life. (*Beat.*) It's ridiculous. Everyone's entitled to a life whatever their circumstances.

JANE. Of course they are.

ANNA. You're so lucky Jane. I need a 'Paul'. But I've never had any luck with men. I am sitting here waiting for Jeremy to ring me like I was twenty-something. (*Beat.*) I envy what you've got with Paul. He's considerate. He does his bit. He's obviously devoted to you. And he's marvellous with Tom: he's genuinely interested. He's a find!

JANE. He's not perfect.

ANNA. But you love being with each other. It's so obvious. (*Beat.*) Mind: I couldn't do with the ragging. My vanity probably, but I couldn't cope with it.

JANE. He's terrible about nicknames. (*Beat.*) There's nothing malicious in it. It's affectionate.

ANNA. I wouldn't have a man in my life calling me 'Lumpy'.

JANE. He's not going to change.

ANNA. It's insulting.

JANE. It isn't serious.

ANNA. I hate nicknames. My brother used to do it to me. It didn't mean anything but it did. (*Beat.*) They're 'taking the piss out of you' names.

JANE. I did look ridiculous.

ANNA. He asked you to put the costume on!

JANE. That's true.

ANNA. And then insulted you. You did look funny but . . . He just likes taking the piss. (*Beat.*) Don't listen to me. It's a bit of a thing for me. I know I don't like them. (*Beat.*) I like being flattered. I'm so vain.

*ANNA's mobile goes.*

My god! That'll be the man. Excuse me.

*She answers.*

Darling. Hold on a second. (*To* JANE.) Why don't you go and open your pressie? I'm dying to see what you think of it.

JANE. Okay. I'll do that.

*She leaves.*

ANNA. I'm back. (*Pause as* ANNA *listens: she starts laughing.*) No I haven't. I wouldn't be seen dead in them. (*Pause: she laughs more: she whispers.*) Wellingtons! Please. (*Beat.*) It's what happens darling, when you've got children; you've got to get on with their friends, and their parents. (*Beat.*) They're very, very kind. Salt of the earth. J.J.'s having a wonderful time. (*Pause.*) I know darling. But they're very useful. They're good for us because they'll always have J.J. Okay? (*Pause.*) So would I sweetheart.

We'd be doing it right now. You know me. (*Pause.*) We would! (*Pause.*) We're just going to have to wait. (*Pause.*) You are my priority. You're my number one. But I've got J.J. too. (*Pause.*) Tomorrow night. We'll be back eight, nine, something like that. (*Pause.*) Can't wait. Love you. (*Pause.*) Bye.

JANE *comes in holding the 'pressie' – an expensive velvet scarf.*

JANE. This is gorgeous Anna. It's beautiful.

ANNA. I thought they were your colours.

JANE. I'd love it whatever colour it was. I've never had anything like this. It's exquisite. (*Beat.*) I feel really pampered.

ANNA. Glad you like it.

JANE. I adore it. I feel terribly spoilt. Paul would never find me something like this. It's the most luxurious thing I've ever been given.

ANNA. I've got a couple. Jeremy gave me them. They're essentials. Put that on and you're dressed up.

JANE. Thank you. I'll treasure it. (*Beat.*) But you really shouldn't have. There was no need.

ANNA. You've given me a fantastic break.

JANE. All the same.

ANNA. Let me see it on you.

JANE *puts it on like you would a warm woolly scarf.* ANNA *gets up to rearrange it. She undoes it and throws it loosely round* JANE*'s neck.*

That's better – more relaxed. Or you can just have it over the shoulder.

*She rearranges it like that.*

It suits you. (*Beat. Pointing.*) Do you do anything about that?

JANE. What?

ANNA. Your hair?

JANE. What hair?

ANNA. Sorry! Big mouth again.

JANE. No. Go on.

ANNA. I just noticed the hair on your upper lip. I'm sorry. I shouldn't have opened my big mouth.

JANE. Do you think it shows?

ANNA. I've never noticed it before.

*Pause.*

JANE. I hate it.

ANNA. It's fine. There really isn't much.

JANE. I don't do anything about it because I don't know what I could do.

ANNA. Then leave it.

JANE. I'm very conscious of it.

ANNA. Don't be. (*Beat.*) Does it bother Paul?

*Pause.*

I shouldn't have said anything.

JANE. I'm glad you did.

ANNA. It's not bad. It's very fine. (*Beat.*) You could do a bit of electrolysis. (*Beat.*) But if it doesn't bother you leave well alone. I'm just hopelessly vain. (*Beat.*) I've spoilt it now. And you love the scarf. Damn. (*Beat.*) Forget I said it. Please.

JANE. Don't worry.

ANNA. It's the curse of the older woman. It's another thing our mothers didn't warn us about. Forties? Facial hair. We've all got it.

*Pause.*

JANE. There are things our mothers didn't dream of. (*Beat.*) I'll put this away.

*She leaves.*

*Blackout.*

**Scene Six**

TOM *and* J.J. *are with their extra maths tutor* BRIAN. *It is Saturday 11.30 a.m. They are standing round the kitchen table at* PAUL, JANE *and* TOM*'s house.* TOM *hands* BRIAN *his homework.*

BRIAN. Thank you Tom.

　　BRIAN *waits for* J.J. *to give him his homework.*

　　J.J.?

J.J. What?

BRIAN. I'm waiting.

J.J. What for?

BRIAN. Your homework.

*Pause.*

J.J. I didn't have time.

BRIAN. Have you done any of it?

J.J. I didn't have time.

BRIAN. So you haven't even started?

　　J.J. *pulls his homework out of his bag and gives it to* BRIAN. BRIAN *sits down.*

J.J. I did a bit and then . . . I haven't finished it. I didn't have time.

BRIAN. I see.

J.J. It takes ages.

BRIAN. How long did it take you Tom?

TOM. Can't remember.

BRIAN. Forty minutes?

TOM. Don't think it was as long as that.

BRIAN. Twenty?

TOM. Something like that.

BRIAN. That's very good Tom. Well done.

*He holds up* TOM*'s homework.*

I set you part of an old exam paper so you could time yourselves and see how you were doing. It should have taken you about twenty minutes. (*Beat.*) I can't see how you're progressing J.J. if you don't bother to do the homework.

J.J. I didn't have time. I . . . I . . .

BRIAN. I'm not interested. You could have done it this morning before you came here. You could have done it last night. Twenty minutes: that's all it would have taken you. Maybe half an hour. (*Beat.*) Could you go and get Jane, Tom.

J.J. I'll do it.

BRIAN. Yes you will. Tom?

TOM *leaves.* BRIAN *looks over* J.J.*'s work.*

You'll do it here with me now. (*Beat.*) You've done a couple of questions. That's a start. '15.30' is three thirty. That's right. And the film would end at let me see . . . let me see . . . Yup: that's right. '16.20'. You can easily do this J.J. Sit down.

J.J. *sits.*

J.J. They were the easy ones.

BRIAN. You score points answering them as well. Everything counts. (*Beat.*) All I'm doing here is helping you get through this examination.

J.J. I can't do the equations.

BRIAN. I'll help you.

J.J. They don't make any sense.

BRIAN. What's a minus and a plus?

J.J. Minus.

BRIAN. Right. Plus and a minus?

J.J. Minus.

BRIAN. Right. Minus and minus?

J.J. Plus. But it doesn't make sense.

BRIAN. Right.

J.J. I know it but when I come to do it I can't do it.

*JANE comes in.*

BRIAN. Jane. Great. Could you possibly put Tom somewhere else so I can have time with J.J. on his own.

JANE. What's happened?

BRIAN. Nothing's happened. I just need to see them separately for half an hour or so.

JANE. What'll Tom do?

BRIAN. Once J.J.'s settled I'll come and give him something.

JANE. Alright.

BRIAN. They'll mess about if they're in here together.

JANE (*to* J.J.). We can't have that can we?

BRIAN. He's got a bit behind. That's all.

JANE. I'll put Tom next door in the sitting room.

BRIAN. Excellent. Tell him I'll be with him in five minutes.

*She leaves.*

Write these things down.

*J.J. gets ready to write.*

Two times two.

J.J. Come on! I'm not stupid.

BRIAN. Two times minus two.

J.J. I can't do it when it's equations.

BRIAN. Come on. We're wasting time. Minus three, plus two, minus four, minus two, plus one, minus one. Equals?

*JANE comes in.*

JANE. Tom wants me to get his things.

BRIAN. Fine. I'll be through in a second. Got that?

*JANE gets TOM's maths books.*

J.J. Yeah.

BRIAN. Sit properly.

*J.J. moves a bit in his chair.*

Two, plus four, minus three, minus two, plus one, minus six. Equals?

*J.J. looks after JANE as she leaves.*

Concentrate J.J.

J.J. I'm doing it.

*BRIAN checks that he is and moves his briefcase to the other side of the table.*

BRIAN. I'll sit over here.

*JANE comes in.*

JANE. I'll see you later then.

*She begins to leave.*

BRIAN. What do you mean?

JANE. I've got to go out.

BRIAN. Now?

JANE. Yes.

BRIAN. Get on with that J.J.

*BRIAN gets up and draws JANE aside.*

I'm not happy with that.

JANE. What are you talking about?

BRIAN. Is there anyone else in the house?

J.J. Done it.

BRIAN. Good. Right.

JANE. There's no one in the house. But my husband's through in the garden.

BRIAN. I didn't realise. I'm sorry.

JANE. Alright?

BRIAN. Absolutely. I . . . Open the back door will you before you go.

*JANE starts to leave.*

And leave it open.

JANE. Do you want me to ask him to come in?

BRIAN. No. I just need to know he's here.

J.J. Done it.

BRIAN. And this. Solve this equation. (*He reads from an exam paper.*)

Baharak cycles from home to work at 8 miles an hour. After work she finds that her cycle has a puncture and walks home at 4 miles per hour.

a) If the distance from home to work is x miles, write down:
   (i) an expression for the time taken to walk home;
   (ii) an expression for the total time she spends travelling.

b) the total time she spends travelling is 3 hours. Write down an expression in x and solve it to find the distance from home to work.

JANE. See you later then. (*Beat.*) Or I probably won't. I'll be more than an hour. So, see you next week.

BRIAN. Okay. Bye.

*JANE goes. BRIAN looks at J.J.'s work.*

That's right. And that. (*Beat.*) Not quite.

*TOM comes in.*

One moment Tom.

*J.J. pulls a face at TOM.*

Cut that out. (*Beat.*) When I come back I'm going to sit right here opposite you until you finish your homework.

*He leaves with TOM.*

*J.J. stands up once they've gone and makes 'wanker' gesture at his back. Stops. Thinks.*

*Blackout.*


### Scene Seven

*The same setting as Scene One, and the same day as the previous scene, later on in the evening. Ten p.m. Loud tech / club music is playing. PAUL and BRIAN are kissing. A deep embrace. They are standing up. BRIAN's overnight bag is at his feet. They let go.*

PAUL. Oh I've been longing for that.

*He wants to kiss again. BRIAN stops him.*

BRIAN. We've got the rest of the weekend.

PAUL. Heaven.

*BRIAN pulls out a chair and sits down.*

BRIAN. I'm knackered.

PAUL *picks up* BRIAN*'s bag and is about to take it upstairs.*

PAUL. Let's . . .

BRIAN. No. Not yet. I need to relax a bit first.

PAUL *puts the bag down, pulls out a chair and sits down.*

PAUL. Have you eaten?

BRIAN. I'm fine. I had a revolting meal at a service station.

PAUL. Poor love.

BRIAN. Could we kill the sounds?

PAUL. Don't you like it?

BRIAN. Not much.

PAUL *turns the music off.*

You're such a maniac about your age.

PAUL. I quite like it.

BRIAN. You're making yourself like it. (*Beat.*) Aren't you?

PAUL. I've got to.

BRIAN. You're fine the way you are.

PAUL. Am I?

BRIAN. Would I be here Paul if I didn't want to be?

PAUL. I've been longing for this.

BRIAN. The only reason you need to get that music is for Tom.

PAUL. You're so sweet.

BRIAN. I mean it. I like you the way you are.

PAUL. The old man.

BRIAN. The older man. (*Beat.*) You're very sexy. (*Beat.*) I've never had a boyfriend like you.

PAUL. So I'm an adventure?

BRIAN. Oh yeah. You're my first married boyfriend.

PAUL. Really?

BRIAN. Obviously I can't know with all the men I've . . .

PAUL. But I'm the first you know is?

BRIAN (*laughing*). Not that you'd ever know.

PAUL. Good.

BRIAN. Have no fears there. You're pretty good in the sack.

PAUL. You too.

BRIAN. And age doesn't come into it.

PAUL. Okay. I've got it.

BRIAN. Be hung up about your age if you want because of Tom but not for me.

PAUL. He's great isn't he?

BRIAN. Delightful.

PAUL. He tries so hard.

BRIAN. Yes he does. He's no high flyer but he certainly tries.

PAUL. Is he . . . ?

BRIAN. We don't talk about our 'other people'.

PAUL. I know.

BRIAN. You don't ask me about Robin. Or tell me about Tom.

PAUL (*laughing*). Robin's your partner. I don't want to know about him.

BRIAN. And Tom's your son and I didn't come down here to talk about how he's getting on with his // maths revision.

PAUL (*interrupts*). 'Course you didn't. (*Beat.*) I just love the lad so much. He's my favourite topic of conversation. I'm besotted.

BRIAN. You've a lot to be proud of.

PAUL. He's gorgeous isn't he?

BRIAN. He's a nice lad.

PAUL. And he's going to be drop dead gorgeous.

BRIAN. He's going to be. He's still a kid.

PAUL. Don't you . . . ?

BRIAN. Please!

PAUL. Sorry.

BRIAN. Never. I have never, ever fallen for a lad. It's not my thing.

PAUL. Nor me. I love watching the changes in him though. Seeing this adult man emerging. It's quite miraculous.

BRIAN. Proud Dad.

PAUL. He's the reason I'm still married.

BRIAN. How do you mean?

PAUL. I don't think now's the right time for me and Jane to separate.

BRIAN. I wouldn't know about that.

PAUL. It's bloody hard.

BRIAN. And none of my business.

PAUL. You're so lucky.

BRIAN. Why?

PAUL. You haven't missed it with 'coming out'.

BRIAN. You've got the best of both worlds. Surely.

PAUL. So long as it lasts.

BRIAN. Why shouldn't it?

PAUL. I have to behave.

BRIAN (*laughing*). So do I. We're both having affairs.

PAUL. Are we?

BRIAN. What do you think I'm doing here?

PAUL. Fantastic.

BRIAN. Having second thoughts?

PAUL. God no. I'm crazy about you.

BRIAN. Good.

PAUL. It's just . . .

BRIAN. What?

PAUL. You say this age thing doesn't matter but it does. It certainly has for me.

BRIAN. Why?

PAUL. Where do I start? Where do I start? (*Beat.*) I'm Catholic.

BRIAN. An evil sodomite.

PAUL. That sort of thing. But it's very real. Still is. I even thought very, very seriously about becoming a priest. (*Beat.*) But I could do it with women. And I didn't want to be gay.

BRIAN. Please.

PAUL. Sorry.

BRIAN. I hope you're not feeling 'bi' here.

PAUL. No way. I just feel like talking a bit. We haven't had this sort of time together before.

BRIAN. Fine.

PAUL. I felt I couldn't come out while my Mum was alive.

BRIAN. That old turkey.

PAUL. It's very real.

BRIAN. When did she die?

PAUL. Year and a half ago.

BRIAN. I'm sorry.

PAUL. It's okay. Do you mind if we talk a bit?

BRIAN. Sure.

PAUL. I feel guilty I never came out while she was alive. She always thought the trouble Jane and I were having in our marriage was Jane's fault. And it was mine.

BRIAN. Does Jane know about me?

PAUL. She knows I'm seeing a boyfriend this weekend.

BRIAN. So she knows . . .

PAUL. I'm bisexual.

BRIAN. Then that's alright.

PAUL. I'm not into dishonesty. But it's . . .

BRIAN. I don't want to know.

PAUL. Okay.

BRIAN. Did she know you got into wind // surfing because . . . ?

PAUL (*interrupts*). We don't talk about our partners.

BRIAN. Touché. (*Beat.*) Come on. We're here to fuck. Show me the way.

BRIAN *stands.*

PAUL. Just let me phone Jane.

*He takes out his mobile. He punches out the number.*

I always phone in and give her a goodnight kiss.

BRIAN. On your weekends off?

PAUL. That's right.

BRIAN. Isn't there a phone here?

PAUL. She can't trace this. She wouldn't like to know we were here. (*To* JANE.) Sweetie hi. Good movie? (*Beat.*) Was it? (*Beat.*) Oh great. You enjoyed it anyway. (*Beat.*) Night, night then. Sleep tight. Kiss. Kiss.

*He puts the phone away. He stands up, picks up* BRIAN*'s bag and moves towards the bedroom.*

Follow me.

*They go towards the bedroom.*

*Blackout.*

## Scene Eight

*The next day.* ANNA*'s home. A couple of things to suggest better, more up-to-date taste would be good:* ANNA *is in property after all.*

ANNA. You swear J.J. that you're telling me the truth?

J.J. Yes.

ANNA. Promise?

J.J. Yes. (*Beat.*) He made Tom go and work in a different room so he could get me on my own.

ANNA. J.J. . . .

J.J. This is so not fair. Why don't you believe me? Tom's Mum wouldn't be doing this to him.

ANNA. That's because Tom doesn't lie to Jane.

J.J. That's what you think.

ANNA. Does Tom lie?

J.J. Why do you always think I'm lying?

ANNA. Oh J.J. darling I don't want to think you're lying but you make it so difficult for me. You've lied so often, I don't know when you're telling the truth anymore.

J.J. You don't always tell the truth. Everyone knows not to trust estate agents.

ANNA. That is enough. You cost me over a hundred pounds stealing my credit card and surfing about through God knows what, so don't you dare try and lecture me about morality.

J.J. I'm not mum. I'm not. I said I was sorry about the money. I'll pay you back one day.

ANNA. J.J., if he really . . . You've got to understand actions have consequences, and if Brian really has done what you say he has done then the consequences will be very serious.

J.J. What will happen?

ANNA. I don't know exactly but far worse than losing a few hundred pounds on a credit card, or receiving some very embarrassing e-mails.

J.J. I'm sorry Mum. I really, really am about the credit card but you've got to believe me.

ANNA. In the middle of the lesson?

J.J. Yeah.

ANNA. In the middle of doing some sort of maths together Brian stopped everything, stopped teaching you and sent Tom somewhere else?

J.J. Yeah.

ANNA. What? He was halfway through a sentence and he told Tom to leave?

J.J. I can't remember. It happened very fast.

ANNA. Okay.

*Pause.*

What led up to him telling Tom to go somewhere else?

J.J. I don't know. He just did it.

ANNA. Because you were messing around?

J.J. We weren't messing around.

ANNA. No. You were messing around.

J.J. I wasn't.

*Pause.*

We hadn't even started.

ANNA. J.J. I love you dearly. I'm your mother. But I know better than anyone you like messing about and you like taking the piss. Wherever and whenever you can.

J.J. Mum I was scared.

ANNA. But up to then you were messing about.

J.J. NO. I told you.

*Pause.*

ANNA. What usually happens?

J.J. I don't know.

ANNA. Yes you do.

J.J. I don't.

ANNA. You're being silly J.J.

J.J. I'm not. He touched me. He's a batty man.

ANNA. A what?

J.J. A bum bandit.

ANNA. Don't be disgusting.

J.J. But he IS.

ANNA. Gay?

J.J. Yeah.

*Pause.*

ANNA. I have to know exactly what happened.

J.J. I've just told you.

*Pause.*

ANNA. Where did he touch you?

J.J. Here.

*He touches his thigh.*

ANNA. Like that?

J.J. What do you mean?

ANNA. He happened to brush your thigh by mistake?

J.J. It wasn't a mistake.

ANNA. All I'm trying to do J.J. is get to the // the bottom of this.

J.J. You don't believe me.

ANNA. I'm not saying that.

J.J. You don't care.

ANNA. Of course I care.

J.J. You don't.

ANNA. J.J. please.

J.J. He's a pervert. He got me there by myself so he could do it.

ANNA. He was sitting beside you?

J.J. Yeah.

ANNA. Right next to you?

J.J. What does it matter? He wanted to stick his hand right in there. He wanted to grab hold of it. He wanted to touch me, feel me, do things. He came over to me and he // stuck his hand . . .

ANNA (*interrupts*). So he wasn't sitting beside you?

J.J. No. He . . .

ANNA. You've got to get this right J.J. He wasn't sitting beside you.

J.J. Tom left and I was sitting at the table. I was there by myself.

ANNA. Okay. I've got that much.

J.J. Why are you making such a fuss? He's a batty boy, a shirt lifter, an AIDS carrier. He's a pervert.

ANNA. Tom had left the room.

J.J. And he came and did it. He came over and did it.

ANNA. Show me.

J.J. You don't believe me.

ANNA. Show me.

J.J. You're my mother.

ANNA. Show me J.J.

> J.J. *goes through the actions of what he is telling* ANNA *took place.*

J.J. He was over at the door.

ANNA. He shut the door?

J.J. Yeah. He shut the door. And he came over to me.

ANNA. Where were you?

J.J. I'm telling you. I'm telling you. Listen!

ANNA. Show me where you were.

J.J. I was sitting at the table with all my stuff.

ANNA. I see.

J.J. And he came over and sat beside me.

ANNA. He pulled up a chair?

J.J. Yeah.

ANNA. Then what?

J.J. I started going over the homework I'd done.

ANNA. What do you mean?

J.J. I was looking at it.

ANNA. Right.

J.J. And he came over and sat beside me and did it.

ANNA. Just like that?

J.J. Yeah.

ANNA. You've never said anything before.

J.J. He's never tried it on before.

ANNA. And you sat there with him till the end of the lesson.

J.J. Something like that.

ANNA. Did he touch you once or more than that?

J.J. What does it matter? He touched me. Filthy pervert had his hand between my legs. // He wanted to keep

ANNA (*interrupts*) Between your legs?

J.J. Yes. He kept it there.

ANNA. You didn't fight him J.J. You didn't scream and run out. You didn't go and tell Jane.

J.J. She wasn't there.

ANNA. You didn't say that before.

J.J. That's the whole point. That's why he went and did it.

ANNA. So there was no one in the house except you and Tom and him.

J.J. Yes. Yes. That's what I'm telling you. Jane had gone shopping. That's why he did it. Because he'd got himself on his own with us. We were all alone in the house.

ANNA. He'd got himself on his own with you once he'd got rid of Tom.

J.J. Yeah so he could touch me up. So he could squash himself up on me and grab my thigh and hold his hand between my legs and squeeze. No he was touching himself. He was wanking. He had his hand on me and he was wanking.

ANNA. Oh Jesus.

J.J. I couldn't do anything. What could I do? I couldn't do anything.

ANNA. And he knew it.

*Blackout.*

### Scene Nine

*The next day.* PAUL *and* JANE*'s house.*

JANE. We've got to decide.

PAUL. I know we have.

JANE. We engaged him.

PAUL. He's a good teacher.

JANE. What difference does that make?

PAUL. I find it so hard to believe.

JANE. I agree there's nothing about Brian that would make you think he was gay.

PAUL. Not every gay man announces it to the world. You don't have to wear it like a badge. This isn't the mincing seventies. This is now.

JANE. I know. If anyone should know that I should. I do. I know.

*Beat.*

PAUL. What difference does it make if Brian's gay or not?

JANE. Don't be stupid Paul.

PAUL. We've no proof J.J.'s telling the truth.

JANE. Why shouldn't he be telling the truth?

PAUL. Has Tom said anything?

JANE. I haven't asked him.

PAUL. And he hasn't said anything?

JANE. No.

PAUL. Well there you are.

JANE. What?

PAUL. Well he was there wasn't he?

JANE. You were in the garden. Brian had separated them.

PAUL. Why?

JANE. Tom says it was because J.J. was messing – Look it doesn't matter. J.J. says Brian –

PAUL. A man like Brian fancying a boy in the privacy of his own head is one thing. But risking his career by – seems mad, unbelievable.

*Beat.*

JANE. Are you saying you think Brian's gay?

PAUL. Of course he is.

JANE. Oh Christ, what a mess. I hire a gay man to give extra maths tuition to two underage teenage boys and you know.

PAUL. Stop it! Stop it, Jane. // This is pernicious rubbish

JANE. Two impressionable, vulnerable teenage // boys for whom I am responsible. One of them is your son.

PAUL. It cannot be allowed to go any further. It's J.J. projecting a fantasy, bearing a grudge because he's a lazy, lying adolescent . . . Anna said it herself. He lies about everything.

*Dialogue overlaps here.*

JANE. Your son could be the victim of an assault.// A criminal assault. In terms of the law J.J. is underage.

PAUL. For Christ sake not every gay man is into little boys. Gay does not mean paedophile. When is the world going to understand –

JANE. According to Anna J.J.'s already sexually active: apparently he's got a girlfriend called Marion. Or was it Monica. She says J.J.'s fifteen going on twenty-something. He's hardly an innocent in short trousers. How can you be so sure he wouldn't be a temptation, underage or not?

*Beat.*

PAUL. Brian wouldn't.

JANE. How do you know?

PAUL. I just do.

JANE. Because you're gay.

PAUL. I'm bisexual.

JANE. When the urge takes you any hole will do.

PAUL. He's not guilty of this.

JANE. How do you know?

*Beat.*

Answer me.

*Beat.*

I know the sort of men Anna goes for because she blathers on about it all the time. How do you know what sort Brian fancies? Brian's here once a week to teach the boys and he won't even take time out to have a coffee. When have you talked to him about anything?

*Silence.*

PAUL. It's a very serious business this for a gay teacher.

JANE. Would you stand up in Brian's defence?

PAUL. The most serious.

JANE. Would you?

PAUL. If I believed him to be innocent, absolutely I would.

JANE. Even though you barely know him? Even though you haven't spoken to him? . . . You would defend him simply because he's a gay man?

PAUL. No.

JANE. So you know somehow, miraculously, by telepathy. by secret language, by winks, by 'gaydar', by some sort of masonic sort of code, some bloody way, you know//

TOM *enters the room.*

TOM. Have you seen my maths book anywhere?

JANE. It's upstairs on the landing.

TOM *leaves.*

PAUL. Are you doing homework?

TOM. Yeah.

PAUL. Give me a shout if you need any help.

TOM. OK. Thanks Dad.

*Beat.*

JANE. How do you know what his sexual tastes are?

PAUL. Keep your voice down can't you?

JANE. How?

PAUL. How?

JANE. Yes. How?

*Beat.*

Why don't you tell me the truth?

*Pause.*

JANE. You must have done something with Brian away from here to know what you know.

*Beat.*

PAUL. Yes.

JANE. You swore to me you wouldn't do that.

PAUL. I couldn't help it.

JANE. Christ Almighty! We've managed to keep this thing going for years.

PAUL. I know.

JANE. I'm not part of the gay Paul. That's your private, secret life. And it musn't have anything to do with me and my home and . . . us as a family.

PAUL. Brian and I met . . .

JANE. I don't want to know anything about Brian. You meet the men you want to fuck . . .

PAUL. I'm trying to explain . . .

JANE. You agreed. I'd never meet them. I'd never be able to put a face . . .

PAUL. You introduced us.

JANE. You bastard.

PAUL. I couldn't . . .

JANE. You know how much this hurts me.

PAUL. Both of us.

JANE. Shut up Paul. Shut up.

PAUL. J.J. can't be right.

JANE. I didn't want to know. Nobody knows about you, us. Our love . . . Our marriage . . . Our children . . . Your gayness . . . (*Cries.*) You promised.

PAUL *goes to touch her.*

DON'T TOUCH ME!

PAUL. No one could have predicted -

JANE. We struck a bargain. And you reneged on it. It was the only rule.

*Blackout.*

### Scene Ten

ANNA*'s home. Preferably kitchen. Upmarket as in Scene Seven. Remains of some sort of supper littering the table. Remains of several bottles in evidence. Vodka. Wine. Maybe brandy or grappa as well.* ANNA *is drunk, vicious, upset and on a roll. She is talking on the telephone to* JANE.

ANNA. And you know the funny thing is, despite the fact that I think he is a despicable human being, who should be reported . . . in fact he should be put on that computer thingy they have . . . yes, that's it, the database wotsit . . . Anyway, despite his despicability I can almost feel sorry for him because I have this feeling about where he's coming from. I bet he was brought up a Catholic. Probably packed off at some idiotically young age like Jeremy to some godforsaken monastery run by devious Jesuitical hypocrites blathering on about children being nearest the Lord, especially if equipped with a penis. I mean everybody knows the Catholic church is riddled with it. Those places are nothing more or less than a paedophile's paradise. They are vile places.

*Slight pause.*

Too bloody right I'm upset and maybe I am being extreme but it's a pretty bloody extreme thing to happen.

*A longish beat.*

Why can't I talk like that? Jesus Jane, don't go all PC on me.

ANNA *takes a large slurp of wine/vodka/whatever.*

I mean, listen, they are absolutely everywhere. The Church. Boy Scouts. The Armed Forces. Well maybe not the R.A.F. But definitely The Marines. Royalty. And as for the telly, you can't turn the sodding screen on without some lispy ponce being all arch and giggly somewhere or other. Hello. Hello. Jane? Jane? Are you there? Oh Fuck. Rung off.

*Silence.* ANNA *is trying desperately not to cry.*

(*Raising her glass to no one in particular.*) You try doing it all on your bloody own.

*A beat or two and* J.J. *appears rather sleepily.*

J.J. Mum. Don't drink any more. Why are you shouting? It's nearly midnight.

ANNA. Oh. J.J. I'm sorry. Give me a hug.

*Blackout.*

## PART TWO

### Scene Eleven

TOM *and* J.J. *are on mountain bikes.* J.J.*'s is flashier and probably newer and more expensive. One or both might be doing wheelies at the top of the scene. They are in a street or maybe some kind of back alley on their way to get a couple of DVDs.*

TOM. Come on, J.J. What's the big deal? What's going on?

J.J. Don't knock it. We're each getting a DVD out of it.

TOM. Yeah, but how come?

J.J. I'm sworn to secrecy.

TOM. You've been watching too much Austin Powers.

J.J. Is that what you fancy getting out then?

TOM. Austin Powers? No. I'd rather have Johnny English.

J.J. Broad beans and bad jokes. That's what my Mum calls it.

TOM. What does she know?

J.J. Not a lot

TOM. Shall we go then?

*Silence.*

TOM *starts to move off.* J.J. *hangs back.*

Come on.

J.J. What's a secret thing you wouldn't want anyone else except a best friend to know?

TOM. What is it with you and secrets?

J.J. If I tell you, you tell me?

TOM. Maybe.

J.J. Promise. I won't tell.

TOM. OK.

J.J. Go on then.

TOM. You first.

J.J. I never slept with Monica. She wouldn't let me. Your turn.

TOM. Do I have to?

J.J. I won't tell.

TOM. I played doctors with Alice's dolls.

*Beat.*

How about we watch *Lord of the Rings* again?

J.J. *Fellowship* or *Two Towers*?

TOM. *Two Towers.*

J.J. I'd rather see *Matrix*.

*Beat*

Tom? Can I ask you something?

TOM. Yeah sure.

J.J. Brian's a batty man, isn't he?

TOM. I don't know, is he?

J.J. Yeah. He is.

TOM. So? He's a good teacher.

*Beat.*

J.J. Would you lie to keep someone out of prison?

TOM. I dunno, J.J. Depends what they'd done I guess. Depends who they were //

J.J. I'd do it for you, Tom.

TOM. I don't know what you're on about, J.J. I'm not going to prison.

J.J. I'm talking about supporting your mates when they're getting grief.

TOM. What've you done?

J.J. I need you to do something for me . . .

TOM. What?

J.J. I need you to back me up.

TOM. About what?

J.J. About Brian?

TOM. What about him?

J.J. He fancies me.

TOM. What?

J.J. He does. He probably fancies you too. You've got to back me up on this.

TOM. What are you talking about?

J.J. The other day he deliberately had you moved into another room.

TOM. Yeah, because you hadn't done your homework. He wanted you to catch up.

J.J. That was just an excuse. He saw the chance of getting me on my own and he couldn't keep his hands off me.

*Pause.*

TOM. You're lying . . .

J.J. You sound like my Mum.

TOM. That's bollocks J.J. It isn't his fault you're crap at maths.

J.J. You're a crap friend.

*Beat.*

I told my Mum.

TOM. Told her what?

*Beat.*

J.J. I told my Mum he touched me up and she believed me.

TOM. Did he?

J.J. He wanted.

TOM. Yeah, but did he? Jesus J.J., what did you do that for?

J.J. I don't know Tom. I just did. I need you to help me Tom.

TOM. You want me to say it's true?

J.J. Yeah it is. Say you saw him doing it to me.

TOM. I can't.

J.J. You can.

TOM. I can't.

J.J. Make it up. Just say . . . he came up close . . . and touched you up.

TOM. Me? He didn't. No way.

J.J. Go on.

TOM. He didn't.

J.J. I know he didn't. But if you said it. Everyone believes you. If you said it had happened to you, they'd believe me.

*Beat.*

And then that would be it then, wouldn't it?

TOM. What?

J.J. He'd have to go, wouldn't he?

TOM. Don't see why, it's not true.

J.J. 'Course he would.

TOM. Why?

J.J. 'Cos we're underage.

*Pause.*

TOM. Bloody hell J.J.

*Beat.*

What have you got against Brian?

J.J. (*interrupts*). What about me? What's everyone got against me? I need you to back me up, Tom. I got Mum to believe me but I don't think Jane will.

TOM. I can't do it. Sorry J.J.

J.J. You don't have to go into detail. Just say you saw him looking at me and . . . You thought it was funny when he sent you out. Something. Come on . . .

TOM. I'm no good at lying.

J.J. It's not difficult.

TOM. I don't want to.

J.J. Please!

TOM. I said I can't do it J.J.

J.J. You're my best mate for fuck's sake.

TOM. You shitforbrains. You stupid wanker. Look I'd like to help you out but I can't tell lies about a gay man touching you up.

J.J. You've just got to say it. He didn't touch // you up but –

TOM. // Jane would never believe me.

J.J. He didn't touch you // but you saw him with me –

TOM. // She wouldn't // believe me.

J.J. Just make it up.

TOM. She'd never, ever believe me.

J.J. Why wouldn't she?

TOM. It just wouldn't do any good.

J.J. It would.

TOM. It wouldn't.

J.J. Why?

TOM. 'Cos Jane's not like that.

J.J. What do you mean?

TOM. She's different about gay men.

J.J. How do you mean?

TOM. She just is.

J.J. I don't understand, Tom.

*Pause.*

TOM. Dad's gay for fuck's sake.

*Beat.*

J.J. Your Dad? Gay? No way.

TOM. He is.

*TOM starts to leave on his bike.*

Come on. Let's get *8 Mile*.

J.J. How come he's gay? (*Calling after* TOM.) Wait, Tom. Mum hates rap.

TOM (*offstage*). *Die Another Day* then. Nobody hates Piers Brosnan.

*Blackout.*

### Scene Twelve

*Morning. The same time as the last scene.* PAUL *and* JANE*'s house. Preferably kitchen.*

ANNA. I expected you to back me all the way on this one Jane.

JANE. All I'm saying is I don't think we should rush into anything without evidence.

ANNA. You mean you don't believe J.J. is telling the truth?

JANE. I'm not saying that Anna, although by your own account he can be economical with it at the best of times.

ANNA. He isn't lying Jane.

JANE. I know I'd want to do the same as you if it had happened to Tom, but it hasn't happened to Tom. Tom didn't even see what happened did he?

*Pause.*

ANNA. You wouldn't by any chance have some paracetamol, would you?

JANE. Yes. I think so. (*Searches in her bag, on a shelf wherever.*) Would you like some more coffee?

ANNA. Don't be cross with me Jane. I was in an awful state.

*Beat.*

Don't you ever get drunk?

JANE. Actually no, I don't. I don't like not being in control of myself.

*Beat.*

ANNA. I expect you think I'm a terrible mother.

JANE. Don't be silly. I'm sure J.J. appreciates you being so upset on his behalf. Boys need to know we love them. Even when they're grown up.

ANNA. It's times like this I find it so hard being on my own. His bloody father's nowhere to be found when he's needed, and I can't turn to Jeremy because J.J.'s so against \\ him. I do so envy you and Paul.

JANE. Anna, it is really important that as few people as possible know anything about what's happened.

ANNA. Oh absolutely.

*Why?*

JANE. For everyone's sake, if for whatever reason J.J. isn't telling the truth.

ANNA. I don't believe I'm hearing this Jane, we can't just do nothing. J.J. seems alright for now, but I'm worried about when the shock wears off . . . The thought of him being damaged mentally for life because some perverted gay child molester has interfered . . . well . . . ugghh . . . it just doesn't bear thinking about.

JANE. We have to consider the facts, Anna. For a start we don't actually know Brian's gay.

ANNA. Of course he's gay. Why else is he fiddling about with teenage boys?

JANE. The two don't necessarily go together. We can't assume they do.

ANNA. My son has been abused by a gay teacher.

JANE. On the face of it, I wouldn't have suspected Brian of any of this.

ANNA. They're the worst sort, the closets. Bloody devious shits. All saville row suits // and regimental ties. You'd be amazed how many city boardrooms . . .

JANE. // That's enough Anna. That isn't going to get us anywhere. Homosexuality isn't actually illegal.

ANNA. But underage sex is. Which is why I think he should be reported to the police. I don't want anyone else's child to be subjected to the same risks as J.J. and Tom.

JANE. Tom hasn't been subjected to anything.

ANNA. Yet.

JANE. Look, Anna, I'm just as concerned about J.J.'s welfare as Tom's but if you go to the police they will have to investigate. Brian may be charged with a sexual assault on a minor and he may be prosecuted but, what's certain is J.J. will have to give evidence.

ANNA. Naturally.

JANE. But it won't end there. His past would be scrutinised as closely as Brian's. Every misdemeanour dredged up and dragged through the courts. We'd all become involved.

Investigating this will take a long time and put an enormous strain on all of us.

ANNA. What are you suggesting?

JANE. I'm not suggesting anything. I'm just saying this could all be enormously stressful. Brian would deny everything to protect his reputation and career. As things stand it would end up just J.J.'s word against Brian's. Either way difficult to prove in a court of law.

ANNA. All I want to do is the right thing for J.J.

JANE. Of course you do.

ANNA. And the right thing for Tom and you – (*Starting to tremble on the edge of tears.*) I feel so responsible. Like it must be my fault. Like I've let J.J. down. Somehow I haven't protected him. I'm a terrible mother. It's so unfair I should be feeling like this. On my own.

*Beat.*

Do you think I'd feel better if I confronted Brian face to face?

*Beat.*

JANE (*offering her more coffee*). Top up?

ANNA. Please. Okay, so maybe we don't report him to the police. I see what you're saying there and maybe we don't tell the agency yet. But we can't just leave it. He's still out there . . . walking around . . . It's . . . too . . . I can't . . . It's all so . . . I mean if you were in my shoes wouldn't you want to confront him?

JANE. I'm not in your shoes.

ANNA. But if you were?

JANE. I'd do what I have done.

*Beat.*

What is absolutely essential is to make sure there is no possibility of any unpleasantness ever happening here.

Which is why I've already contacted North London Tutors with a view to getting Brian replaced by a woman teacher.

ANNA. But how do we know she won't turn out to be some sex-starved deviant with a penchant for teenage testosterone? Like that Australian weirdo. Or was she South African? Anyway her. Do you remember the case?

JANE. Anna be serious, this is totally beside the point. Mrs Streatfield is in her fifties. She's highly qualified, very experienced and she comes highly recommended.

ANNA. Which is just what you told me about Brian.

JANE. Yes Anna I did. Brian's credentials were impeccable.

*Beat.*

As are Mrs Streatfield's. And Tom and J.J. still need help with their GCSE maths.

*Beat.*

ANNA. What did you actually say to the NLT? Didn't they want to know why?

JANE. I didn't let them get that far. I didn't explain. I just presented it as a fact. If they had pressed me I was just going to say something like there seemed to be a bit of an issue with the boys about male authority figures, so a woman might be a better option. Which is what we've got. She'll be here next Saturday and we need never see Brian Patterson again.

ANNA. But doesn't he need to know why he's been sacked? Otherwise he'll just go on doing it.

JANE. Whatever 'it' was.

*Beat.*

I really don't feel any need to justify my actions to Brian.

*Pause.*

ANNA. I can't help feeling guilty about J.J. I feel as if I owe it to him to do something.

JANE. We have done something.

ANNA. I'll confront Brian with what he has done!

JANE. What will you do? Scream abuse at him? Scratch his eyes out? Kick him in the balls? *You* might feel better. But where would it get you?

ANNA. You really don't think I would be letting J.J. down?

JANE. I think you would be doing him an enormous favour by leaving well alone.

ANNA. I'll break the news to him, then. Mrs . . .

JANE. Mrs Streatfield. He's got a tough lady to deal with in her, apparently.

ANNA. I'll tell him Mr Patttterson won't be coming back.

We're still friends, aren't we Jane?

JANE. Of course we are, don't worry.

*Blackout.*


### Scene Thirteen

*The same day.* PAUL *and* JANE*'s house.*

JANE. I don't understand why we're having this row.

PAUL. You've just gone straight ahead and sacked him!

JANE. I've arranged for someone to replace him.

PAUL. But he won't know why.

JANE. That's not my concern.

PAUL. He's got to know.

JANE. It's a Saturday morning job. A part-time extra. It'll mean nothing to him.

PAUL. You haven't paid him off, have you?

JANE. No of course I haven't. But I was quite prepared to.

PAUL. Brian's bound to ask me what's been going on?

JANE. Well, you tell him if you feel it's so bloody important.

PAUL. Of course it's important.

JANE. Important to whom? To him? Because he cares about you? Do you still care about him? Do you? More than you care about me? Well? Do you?

PAUL. Jane, for God's sake this isn't about us or my relationship with Brian. Brian is a professional teacher. As a professional teacher his good name is everything and he might be about to lose it along with his livelihood.

JANE. All I've done is to tell North London Tutors we no longer require his services.

PAUL. The man's done nothing wrong.

JANE. He may not have.

PAUL. He hasn't!

JANE. O.K. Maybe he hasn't. But you have.

PAUL. So this is all because of that?

*Beat.*

JANE. Yes. Obviously.

PAUL. How do I tell him that?

JANE. That's up to you. I see no reason why he should be affected by this in any way.

PAUL. He's lost his job.

JANE. His Saturday morning job.

PAUL. Extra cash, which he could // really do with . . .

JANE. // So you've had little chats about that as well.

PAUL. This is grossly // unfair.

JANE. I don't want to know about Brian. He hasn't been damaged in anyway.

PAUL. You don't know that. Not yet. You cannot know that for certain . . .

JANE. I have dealt with this. End.

*Beat.*

PAUL. Just because the man's gay. It's absurd.

JANE. Don't start.

PAUL. It's ridiculous.

JANE. What?

PAUL. It's ridiculous.

JANE. What?

PAUL. The whole thing.

JANE. Our marriage? Brian? Unloved little J.J.? Pocket money? Extra maths? What else?

PAUL. We are not talking about our marriage.

JANE. It's what this is all about for me.

PAUL. Why?

JANE. We've been over this a million times.

PAUL. All I want is for Brian to understand the real reasons why he's lost his job. I'm not being unreasonable.

JANE. Why suddenly the whole bloody earth has to move in sympathy with Brian God alone knows. I won't be part of it. It isn't fair.

PAUL. I don't understand why you feel so threatened. We're still here. We have the same lives. We'll just carry on.

*Pause.*

We owe Brian an explanation.

JANE. It's me you owe.

BRIAN. Oh, come on Jane. You're being impossible.

JANE. How dare you?

*Silence.*

Alright. Do it. Explain. Just keep it the hell away from me.

BRIAN. What shall I say?

JANE. You're a big boy. Say whatever you like. Blame me. 'My wife is so neurotic. She thought I was bonking the guy who does the car but found out I was bonking the tutor instead.'

PAUL. I only said the guy who does the car // was a nice looking . . .

JANE (*interrupts*). I don't care. None of this would be happening if you hadn't broken the rule.

PAUL. You're so inflexible.

*Pause.*

Gordon's wife . . .

JANE. Christ! I never met the bloody woman. I never knew Gordon. All he was to me was your first. The first I knew about. Gordon's the beginning. Don't go on about Gordon.

PAUL. She was such an understanding woman.

JANE. Don't you believe it. She'd probably watched him going out to do God knows what with God knows who before you came along.

PAUL. She liked me.

JANE. She was his wife! How could she possibly like you? She was just glad he wasn't indulging every weekend in what do you call it? . . . anonymous sex. Masses and masses and masses of anonymous sex. Swarming about // fucking each other like . . .

PAUL (*interrupts*). You don't know anything about it.

JANE. No I don't. Thank God. Because it hasn't got anything to do with me. Until you go and push my face in it.

PAUL. I couldn't help it.

JANE. You've got to. Or the whole thing'll fall apart.

*Pause.*

PAUL. I'll explain it to him.

JANE. Brian. Brian. Brian. I'm the most important person in this. I am me. I am. // I'm the one that's been hurt.

PAUL. You've got your way.

JANE. I did the right thing for the family. To keep us together.

PAUL. It's always got to be your way.

JANE. I dealt with it immediately. To keep the peace. Where are the thanks? (*Beat.*) I deserve a medal.

*Blackout.*

### Scene Fourteen

BRIAN *and* PAUL *in an old-fashioned wine bar.*

PAUL. You're still shaking.

BRIAN. Wouldn't you be?

PAUL. Here. Drink this. (*Indicating brandy.*). You need to phone Anna. Give me your phone I'll punch her number in for you.

*He takes* BRIAN*'s phone.*

BRIAN. Why would he – I just don't \\ understand.

PAUL. He's a mixed-up kid. I don't suppose he knows why himself.

BRIAN. Homophobic little bastard . . .

PAUL. I know.

BRIAN. No you don't.

*Beat.*

How can you?

PAUL *hands* BRIAN *the phone.*

BRIAN. You think she'll talk to me? Get real.

PAUL. Give it a go. You can tell her I was there in the garden the whole time and I heard nothing. Tell her I'll vouch for that on oath.

BRIAN. You phone her. She'd listen to you.

PAUL. Tell her Tom witnessed everything you said for Christ's sake. Emphasise you only stayed after Jane left because you knew \\ I was there.

BRIAN. You phone her.

PAUL. I don't want Anna to think that we – For Jane's sake. She doesn't want anyone to know.

BRIAN. This isn't about Jane. This is about me.

PAUL. Look I'm your witness. So is Tom. Nothing happened. She has to believe you. Just give her a ring –

BRIAN. And if she won't?

*Pause.*

PAUL. You can tell her to phone me. \\ Look, I've got to go, Jane's expecting me home

BRIAN. Okay give me the phone.

PAUL. You won't say anything about us will you?

BRIAN. The phone please.

PAUL. Please Brian. Promise me.

BRIAN. Give me my phone.

PAUL *hesitates, they look at each other.*

Trust me.

PAUL *gives it to him. And leaves.*

What's the number?

PAUL (*off*). It's in the phone.

BRIAN (*dials* ANNA's *number*). Hullo. Hullo. Mrs Faulkner? It's Brian Patterson. Please don't hang up. We need // to talk.

I knew it.

*He redials the number.*

Not there. Leave a message. Ring Paul. Ask him. He knows.

**Scene Fifteen**

ANNA's *house.* BRIAN, ANNA *and* J.J. *are standing in the kitchen.*

*A long silence.*

J.J. Tell him to go away Mum. I'm scared.

ANNA. It's OK. Just tell Mr Patterson what happened.

J.J. He knows what he did.

BRIAN. If you won't talk to me J.J. you'll soon be talking to the police.

*Silence.*

Tell me what you told your mother. What did you call me? Hmnn? You told her I was gay, didn't you? True I am.

J.J. You see? I told you. Get him away from me.

BRIAN. You should be ashamed of yourself. What else did you say?

ANNA. If you're telling the truth J.J. there's nothing to worry about.

BRIAN. It's not so easy face to face, is it?

*Beat*

You said I molested you, didn't you? Didn't you?

J.J. Yes.

BRIAN. You're a liar J.J.

J.J. Prove it.

BRIAN. I intend to. Sit down.

J.J. Why?

BRIAN. Just sit down at the table please.

J.J. Why should I do anything you want?

ANNA (*loudly*). J.J. please.

> J.J. *reluctantly sits down.*

BRIAN. Is that where you were sitting at the last maths lesson?

J.J. No.

BRIAN. Where were you then?

J.J. In Paul and Jane's kitchen.

BRIAN. Don't try and be clever J.J. Where did you sit at the last maths lesson.

J.J. On the other side of the table.

BRIAN. With your back to the wall?

J.J. Yes.

BRIAN. Would you sit there now, please.

J.J. Mum!

ANNA. It's OK. Just do it J.J.

BRIAN. Where was Tom?

J.J. When?

BRIAN. At the start of the lesson.

J.J. He was with me.

BRIAN. Did he stay there for the whole lesson?

J.J. No.

BRIAN. How many times did he leave the room?

J.J. Not sure.

BRIAN. You're not sure. It was twice, wasn't it.

J.J. If you say so.

BRIAN. Actually it was three. The first time to get Jane.

J.J. Mum. He's a pervert.

ANNA. That's enough, J.J.

BRIAN. He came back with Jane and went out with her again and then Jane came back in and then went out.

J.J. He's trying to confuse me, Mum. \\ It happened then.

ANNA. When?

BRIAN. How could anything have happened then J.J.? Jane came back in a third time almost immediately and said she was going out. That's an awful lot of to-ing and fro-ing, don't you think?

J.J. It's not fair Mum, he knows when it happened.

BRIAN. Where was Paul, when Jane left J.J.?

J.J. How should I know?

BRIAN. He was in the garden, wasn't he? Wasn't that what Jane said.

*No answer.*

Come on, J.J. As Jane was leaving she told us Paul was in the garden. I made sure we weren't alone. I followed the agency's guidelines. They recommend there's always someone else in the house. Answer the question. Where was Paul?

J.J. I don't know. He was outside. He could have gone away?

ANNA. Was the back door open, J.J.?

BRIAN. Yes.

ANNA. J.J.?

J.J. I can't remember?

ANNA. And Tom was in the room next door?

BRIAN. Yes. But there's no door between the two rooms, is there J.J.?

J.J. (*no answer*).

BRIAN. So where was I?

J.J. What do you mean?

BRIAN. Where was I standing?

J.J. When?

BRIAN. When I came back from giving Tom his homework, where did I come to in the room?

J.J. Sort of . . . just about . . . about where you are now.

BRIAN. Here? (*Moving closer.*) Or here? Where? Wherever I stood I was between two wide open doors. Anyone could have seen me.

J.J. He's admitting it, Mum.

BRIAN. What J.J.? What am I admitting to? What might Tom and Paul have seen? What did I do to you?

J.J. I can't say it. \\ Help me Mum.

BRIAN. Can't say what J.J.? Because I didn't do anything? Is that what you can't say.

*Beat.*

Answer me J.J. What did I do?

J.J. (*struggling for words*). You . . . you . . .

BRIAN. Did I come to the right of you? Or was it the left? Did I sit on the table. Go under the table? Did I move the table?

*Silence.*

It didn't happen, did it J.J.? You made it all up. You told a lie.

*Beat.*

You're a liar J.J. Aren't you? A liar!

J.J. *eventually nods.*

*Silence.*

ANNA. I'm horrified with you J.J. Horrified. Do you hear?

J.J. Yeah. Yeah. Yeah.

ANNA. Don't you dare start that.

BRIAN. Do you understand what you've done J.J.?

J.J. I just said you did something when you didn't.

BRIAN. You slandered me J.J. You told a monstrous lie about me behind my back. I could have lost my livelihood.

JANE. How could you, J.J.? How could you do such a thing? How could you be so stupid?

J.J. Don't keep saying I'm stupid.

BRIAN. I'm not the first gay teacher this has happened to. I'm not the first *teacher.* I won't be the last no doubt. Do you know what a bigot is J.J.?

J.J. I'm not stupid.

BRIAN. But are you a bigot J.J.?

ANNA. Of course he's not a bigot Mr Patterson.

BRIAN. A bigot is an intolerant moron who hates anybody they take to be different from themselves, Just for being different. They are stupid, ignorant, pig-headed people. There are a lot of them about and they can be very dangerous.

*Beat.*

Why do you hate me J.J.?

ANNA. I don't think he hates you Mr Patterson.

BRIAN. Who does he hate then, Mrs Faulkner?

*Beat.*

Who else have you lied to J.J.?

J.J. (*no answer*).

ANNA. Tell him J.J.

BRIAN. Your Mum?

　J.J. *nods.*

　And Jane?

ANNA. I told Jane.

BRIAN. And she told Paul. Anyone else?

J.J. (*no answer*).

ANNA. J.J.!

J.J. Tom.

BRIAN. You told Tom, did you? And what did Tom say?

J.J. He wouldn't believe me.

ANNA. I've told you over and over again, not to tell lies.

J.J. You lie.

ANNA. How dare you?

J.J. You do. You lie to me all the time

ANNA. Don't you dare speak to me like that.

BRIAN. Mrs Faulkner // I think perhaps . . .

ANNA. No. Please. Wait a minute. What are you talking about J.J.?

J.J. You don't tell me things.

ANNA. That isn't lying J.J.

J.J. It's just as bad.

ANNA. It isn't.

J.J. It is.

BRIAN. Perhaps it would // be better if we . . .

ANNA. I don't know what he's talking about.

J.J. Why didn't you tell me about Dad // and Beatrix . . .

ANNA (*interrupts*). We're not going to talk about it now.

J.J. You should have told me.

ANNA. We're not talking about this now J.J.

BRIAN. I really do think // we are getting

J.J. You never talk // about anything . . .

ANNA. Don't interrupt! You're going to apologise to Mr Patterson. And you're going to apologise to me.

ANNA. What for?

ANNA. For lying to me. I'll never know when to believe you now.

*Silence.*

J.J. Sorry.

ANNA. Who was that for?

J.J. I've said I'm sorry. Can I go now?

BRIAN. You know something J.J., I don't believe you. I think you're sorry you got found out. I think you're sorry you've got yourself into a lot of trouble. In short you're very sorry for yourself right now but I don't think you give a damn about anybody else's feelings.

*Silence.*

What had you got against me?

*Silence.*

It was downright vindictive J.J.

*Beat.*

J.J. I didn't do it on purpose to make life bad for you.

BRIAN. Imagine being slashed with a stanley knife J.J. An extra sharp, extra strong razor blade slicing into you. Not once but many times. Imagine that J.J. Can you?

*Beat.*

That's how I feel. That's what you've done to me.

*Silence.*

ANNA. I can't believe I was idiotic enough to believe him now but he was so insistent.

BRIAN. I racked my brain for something I had done that you might have taken the wrong way.

J.J. I'm really sorry I've messed you about.

BRIAN. You can't mess about with people like that J.J.

ANNA. You stupid, stupid, stupid boy!

J.J. Don't keep saying I'm stupid.

BRIAN. You understand, don't you J.J.?

J.J. She's always saying it.

BRIAN. That's not what I'm saying J.J.

J.J. She thinks I am. But I'm not. I get hurt too.

BRIAN. I know you do. I accept your apology J.J. I forgive you but I'll never come back and I'll never forget. I hope you don't either. (*Getting up to go.*) Good bye.

ANNA. If it's any consolation Brian I didn't even realise you were gay.

BRIAN. Why should you have known? I'll see myself out.

*He leaves.*

ANNA. Christ I need a drink! You bloody well better have learned your lesson J.J.

*Beat.*

J.J. Why didn't you tell me Beatrix is going to have a baby.

ANNA. How do you know that?

J.J. Dad wrote and told you to tell me.

ANNA. And you read the letter.

*Silence.*

You don't read my letters. You do not go through my purse. You don't take money. You don't help yourself.

J.J. You don't do what you should.

ANNA. Why was it up to me? Why should your Dad expect me to tell you?

J.J. I don't know but he did. And you didn't.

ANNA. I forgot.

J.J. I'm going to have a baby brother or sister and you forgot!

ANNA. Your father should have told you. // He's the one with the new life, the new marriage.

J.J. You forgot. You're my mother and you forgot.

ANNA. I was annoyed with him.

J.J. And you took it out on me.

ANNA. Don't look at me like that.

J.J. Like what?

ANNA. Like you hate me.

J.J. Apologise.

ANNA. I was very angry with your father and jealous.

J.J. And you took it out on me. Apologise.

*Beat.*

ANNA. I'm sorry darling.

J.J. Don't say 'darling'. I hate it.

*Pause.*

ANNA. You'll be spending the weekend with your Dad // so you can –

J.J. (*interrupts*). And Beatrix.

ANNA. And Beatrix. So you can talk to both of them. (*Beat.*) Can't you?

J.J. And you can fuck Jeremy 'cos I won't be in your way.

ANNA. You can be so unkind J.J. Right now I'd love a little of what Jane's got with Paul.

J.J. You wouldn't.

ANNA. To be able to share all this with someone who understands my feelings.

J.J. Paul's gay.

ANNA. Oh, don't be so stupid.

J.J. He is.

ANNA. Stop lying J.J.

J.J. I'm not lying and I'm not stupid.

*He runs out*

ANNA. What have I done now? J.J. darling? Tell me?

*Blackout.*

## Scene Sixteen

PAUL *and* JANE*'s house. Saturday morning. Kitchen.* ANNA, *in a rush on her way to work, is dropping off* J.J. *for the first lesson with Mrs Streatfield.* ANNA *and* JANE *are having coffee.*

ANNA. So. There we are. A pretty chastening experience all round. Especially for J.J.

JANE. Let's hope he's learned his lesson.

ANNA. Mind you, I do feel very sorry for him.

JANE. J.J.?

ANNA. No, no. Brian. He was really devastated.

JANE. Well he's not coming back here.

ANNA. No, I know. Well, not immediately anyway. // I was just thinking it would actually be?

JANE. I don't want him back, Anna. It's not the right thing right now. If you want to do your own thing, well fine. But I am certainly not going to re-employ the man.

ANNA. Oh no, I don't want do anything like that but it is a bit ironic in a way though, isn't it? I mean Tom always liked Brian more than J.J. anyway and Paul thought he was OK too, didn't he?

JANE. Has Paul been talking to you about Brian?

ANNA. No, no. I just meant that when Brian first phoned me, to demand I see him, he made it clear that Paul would back him up.

JANE. I see. Look Anna // I don't want to rush you

ANNA. What do you think Paul's take is on all this. Pretty supportive I should imagine. Given the job he does. Poor man. He must need all the support he can get. Thank God we don't have to live like that. Imagine it, living your everyday life meeting people all day long, not knowing what they might be thinking about you because you are different to them?

JANE. We're all different, Anna.

ANNA. Oh vive la différence. That's what I say. I mean I do have gay friends, well acquaintances and colleagues anyway, perfectly decent blokes, // nothing wrong with their sexuality

JANE. // Do you? I don't.

ANNA. Don't what?

JANE. Have much acquaintance with the gay world.

ANNA. Oh. Right. Well, all I'm trying to say is that sexually speaking I've always thought of myself as very open-minded. //

*ANNA's phone bleeps to indicate text message.*

JANE. Mrs Streatfield will be here // any minute and I better

ANNA. One sec.

*She gets her phone from her bag to have a look.*

Where was I? Oh yes. Same sex partners. If that's your bag. Fine. Doesn't mean deviant, but, unlike you and Paul I couldn't help jumping to conclusions, thinking he must've have, mustn't he?

JANE. What are you talking about, Anna?

ANNA (*referring to phone*). Bloody hell, that's going to be tight. Sorry, what was that?

JANE. Who must've what?

ANNA. Who? Oh right. When J.J. said what he said and you said he was gay –

JANE. Who was gay?

ANNA. Brian of course. It scares me Jane. When I think what I thought. You didn't rush to judgement, did you? Deep down you're a much nicer person than me. You accepted he was gay but not that the other followed. You had the capacity to empathise and I suppose the same goes for Paul.

JANE. You've lost me Anna. Empathise with what?

ANNA. Maybe it's a nature-nurture thing. I don't believe it's genetic, do you?

ANNA*'s phone rings. She answers.*

Hello? Oh hello. Good morning. Aren't we lucky with the weather. What's that? No, no. Left into Beechgrove Avenue. And it's Number Ten. Thank you. Bye. Sorry Jane. I'll have to dash. This is a five-bed des res and could mean monster commission.

JANE. I'll say hello to Mrs Streatfield for you.

ANNA. Thank you darling. Thank you so much for organizing everything. You know you really have been brilliant. (*Shouting off to* J.J.) J.J., I'm going. Wish me luck. I'll pick you up in a couple of hours.

*As she goes*

When can we talk? We must talk? Let's go out.

J.J. *and* TOM *enter.*

JANE. We will. Soon. Bye.

J.J. Don't be late, Mum I don't want to miss the train.

ANNA (off). You won't.

*J.J. and* TOM *sit in silence at opposite ends of the large kitchen table.*

*The boys sort themselves out.* JANE *tidies up.*

TOM. Where are you going?

J.J. Dad's – (*Beat.*) His wife's having a baby.

TOM. When?

J.J. That's the secret Mum wouldn't tell me. You know when we were on the beach.

*The doorbell rings*

TOM. Why?

J.J. It's going to be a little girl. I don't know, she just forgot.

TOM. Sisters are great.

J.J. Deep down, I guess she doesn't like the idea.

TOM. Did your Mum leave your Dad or your Dad leave your Mum?

JANE *comes back in interrupting*

JANE. Tom. J.J. Leave your books where they are. Take your bikes or the football to the common for half an hour.

TOM. What's the matter Mum?

J.J. (*overlapping*). What's going on?

JANE (*interrupting*). Just do as I ask, please? Out of the back door.

*They leave puzzled by the back door.*

BRIAN *comes in to the kitchen carrying a briefcase. All prepared for another maths lesson. A brief awkward pause.*

I'm very sorry about this Mr Patterson, but there seems to be some mistake. Would you mind if I phoned NLT?

BRIAN. Mistake? At the beginning of the week they called me to let me know that you no longer required my services. You wanted a maths tutor still, but not me. They wouldn't give any explanation but suggested that I might like to find another agency. Then two days later your husband phones the agency to say that you have decided not to dispense with my services after all.

*Long beat.*

JANE. We were expecting Mrs Streatfield.

BRIAN. I'm afraid I don't know Mrs Streatfield but I'm sure, like all the teachers on NLT's books she'll be highly competent.

JANE. This has got nothing to do with competence.

BRIAN. What has it got to do with Mrs Patterson?

JANE. Look, I'm sorry but as far as we –

BRIAN. You Mrs Patterson.

JANE. Yes, Brian as far as I am concerned you will not be teaching here again.

BRIAN. Mr Fox has paid me.

JANE. In advance?

BRIAN. We're all paid up.

JANE. I see.

*Beat.*

BRIAN. Please give Tom and J.J. my best. I wish them both luck with their exams. I'll see myself out.

*He leaves.* JANE *sits down at the kitchen table. She is motionless for some long seconds. Then she cradles her head on her arms and starts to silently sob.*

*Blackout.*

### Scene Seventeen

BRIAN *has arranged to meet* PAUL *in a park.* PAUL *is upset and lost for words.*

PAUL. Then I'll never see you again.

BRIAN. Perhaps not.

PAUL. Oh God.

BRIAN. It was bound to happen.

PAUL. But we could –

BRIAN. I don't want to. I'm sorry.

PAUL. I love you.

BRIAN. I'm sorry.

PAUL. I do.

BRIAN. I'm sorry.

PAUL. Don't do this. You've got an open relationship. You're alright about it. That's how you live. That's what you've got an agreement with your partner for. You both have . . . Why?

BRIAN. I can't answer that.

PAUL. Don't do this.

BRIAN. I'm sorry Paul. I just don't want to go on with it.

PAUL. But we were great with each other.

BRIAN. We had some nice times.

PAUL. Why?

BRIAN. It was always going to be short lived. We had a little affair. That's all.

PAUL. What am I going to do? I love you.

BRIAN. I can't help that.

PAUL. I thought you loved me.

BRIAN. Don't turn this into a bloody opera.

PAUL. What the hell am I going to do? I spend the time in between seeing you looking forward to seeing you.

BRIAN. I'm sorry.

PAUL. Is it because I didn't support you enough? I asked them to reinstate you. // I paid you in advance.

BRIAN (*interrupts*). It's not because of anything. I just don't want to carry on with it. You were never my relationship. My life is with Robin and I felt like a fling.

PAUL. You can't . . .

BRIAN. Grow up Paul.

PAUL. I can't stand it. I love you.

BRIAN. Stop saying that.

PAUL. I do.

BRIAN. Your wife is a very nice woman and I don't like hurting her. She doesn't want to know who your boyfriends are but it works the other way as well. I'm uncomfortable that I know her. It was stupid Paul. It was a stupid, stupid thing to do.

PAUL. Don't say that.

BRIAN. I don't know how you live your life at all but I know I don't want to be involved in it. I don't want to have anything to do with it.

PAUL. She understands.

BRIAN. What?

PAUL. I need you.

BRIAN. I'm not in love with you Paul. That's it.

PAUL. You've got to . . .

BRIAN. I haven't. I don't have to do anything.

PAUL. No. But . . .

BRIAN. You're acting like a bloody teenager.

PAUL. I'm sorry.

BRIAN. You've got to work out what you're going to do with your life. You want to be with a man. It's obvious. I can't help you. You've got a lovely wife. Shit! It's impossible. Why you married is beyond me. But you did and you've got to live with it. (*Beat.*) Get somebody else. You've had other partners, other boyfriends. That's the life you've chosen and it's going to be like this.

PAUL. It's unbearable.

BRIAN. I can't help that.

PAUL. Do you think I'll . . . ?

BRIAN. What?

PAUL. I'm going to miss you.

> BRIAN *starts to go. He turns.* PAUL *looks at his feet.* BRIAN *goes.*
>
> *Blackout.*

### Scene Eighteen

PAUL *and* JANE's *house.*

JANE. I thought you were just going to tell him what happened.

PAUL. I did. // And since nothing did happen I assumed

JANE. You went behind my back.

PAUL. What do you mean?

JANE. I don't believe we're having this conversation: I really don't.

PAUL. You started it.

JANE. I'd made other arrangements.

PAUL. Without telling me.

JANE. Why did I have to tell you?

PAUL. We didn't discuss it.

JANE. We haven't discussed things for years.

PAUL. We should.

JANE. I couldn't believe it when I opened the door to him.

PAUL. He's a very good teacher.

JANE. That's not what this is about.

PAUL. It is what it's about.

JANE. It isn't.

PAUL. You're annoyed because // for once you haven't got your own way.

JANE. Got my own way?

PAUL. Yes.

JANE. You think I've been 'getting my own way' all this time?

PAUL. You've made the rules. Your inflexible, draconian rules.

JANE. Which have kept us together as a family.

PAUL. If you can call how we live, being together.

JANE. We have kept it together, haven't we?

PAUL. We haven't been together // for years.

JANE. Who haven't?

PAUL. You and me.

JANE. Whose fault is that?

PAUL. I am not to bloody blame for this.

JANE. I suppose I am.

*Silence.*

What do you want from me?

PAUL. I don't know.

JANE. You're a homosexual man which means you have to have male partners. I've made that possible for you.

PAUL. I have to skulk off // to see a man . . .

JANE (*interrupts*). With you being able to go and see the men you wanted to see as and –

PAUL. When you let me out.

JANE. You are married to me. All I want, all I have ever wanted was for things to carry on as usual for the sake of the kids, for all our sakes for that matter and it has worked.

PAUL. I've had to make it work.

JANE. And I have. I haven't wanted to spend all that time on my own, you know I haven't wanted to take myself off to the movies on your weekends so that you can be with your boyfriends.

PAUL. I always phone you.

JANE. To see how I liked the movie.

PAUL. You've never complained about that before.

JANE. I'm not complaining about it now.

PAUL. I thought you liked me doing that.

JANE. I did.

PAUL. So what are you saying?

JANE. You've changed it.

PAUL. Broken the rule?

JANE. If you want to put it like that.

PAUL. It's not my fault you've been to so many movies on your own.

JANE. No. I could have been having affairs too.

PAUL. I wouldn't have minded.

JANE. I've had the children to look after.

PAUL. Alice has been off our hands for years.

JANE. I've still got Tom.

PAUL. I think you could have had more of a private life than you've chosen to have.

JANE. I didn't choose for my husband to decide years into my marriage he actually wanted to have sex with men.

PAUL. Do you want to go to bed?

JANE. What?

PAUL. Do you want to go to bed?

JANE. Now?

PAUL. Yes now; in the middle of the afternoon.

JANE. We're talking.

PAUL. We could talk in bed. Tom's not here.

Do you want to go to bed? I do love you.

JANE. What do you mean you love me? You don't even notice me.

PAUL. Don't say that.

JANE. It's true.

PAUL. I love you very much.

JANE. You can't Paul.

PAUL. I do.

*Pause.*

JANE. What colours suit me?

PAUL. What?

JANE. What are my colours? What would you say my colours were? When you're thinking of buying me something what do you look for?

PAUL. Something you might like.

JANE. Blues? Browns? Reds? Black?

PAUL. Er yes. I mean . . . You wear lots of colours.

JANE. But which do you think suit me?

PAUL. You look very nice.

JANE. When did you last buy me something that you thought suited me?

PAUL. I find buying you clothes very difficult.

JANE. 'Cos I'm such a lumpy shape. Mrs 'Lumpy'.

PAUL. That was just a joke.

JANE. To you.

PAUL. You didn't mind.

JANE. You didn't think I minded.

PAUL. You didn't say anything.

JANE. I never do.

PAUL. If you were offended you should have said.

JANE. I never say anything. (*Beat.*) We live a bloody lie.

PAUL. I do care for you.

JANE. Which is different from loving someone.

*Pause.*

Something must have happened.

You're only ever interested in sex with me when // you're not getting it.

PAUL. You are my wife.

*Beat.*

It was only a suggestion.

JANE. You've lost the boyfriend so you'll fuck the wife instead.

*Pause.*

The bearded lady. Your lumpy wife. You make me feel hideous.

PAUL. What do you mean bearded?

JANE. You've never noticed have you?

PAUL. What?

JANE. That I have facial hair.

PAUL. Look, I simply asked if you wanted to go to bed. It's not a crime. We are married after all.

JANE. That's right. I could be wearing a bag over my head for the amount you notice me.

PAUL. You're an attractive woman.

JANE. But not to you.

PAUL. You are.

JANE. Well I don't want to go to bed with you. How can I possibly want to when I know I don't satisfy you sexually? How can I possibly want to when I know it's a chore?

PAUL. Don't say that.

JANE. Why not when it's how I feel?

*Pause.*

How long did your affair go on?

PAUL. You don't want to know that.

JANE. No I don't.

PAUL. You don't want to know about my private life.

JANE. Your life which was private till now.

PAUL. My life which my wife wouldn't talk about.

JANE. Couldn't talk about.

PAUL. Refused to acknowledge.

JANE. Had to keep within the confines of the marriage.

PAUL. Decided that was the way she was going to have it.

JANE. Had to have it.

PAUL. Which is why we are where we are now.

JANE. Which doesn't suit anyone.

*Pause.*

PAUL. What do you want to do?

JANE. What's right for Tom.

PAUL. And what's right for us.

JANE. I don't know what's right for us.

PAUL. Maybe Tom will know.

*Blackout.*

### Scene Nineteen

*Heather Cottage. A day or so later.* PAUL, JANE *and* TOM *have all been out for a walk. Aftermath of tea. Debris of cups. Remains of toasted muffins.* JANE *and* PAUL *could be washing up.* TOM *is doing something upstairs.*

PAUL. So, what do you think?

JANE. I find it all so sad.

PAUL. It's not the end of the world Jane.

JANE. Easy for you to say

PAUL. It's what he wants.

JANE. He could be just trying to please us. Because he thinks that now Alice has left home more or less, you and I are being forced to stay together because of him. He's made himself the problem.

PAUL. He gets to share his time with both of us.

*Silence.*

JANE. You are so unfeeling.

PAUL. I'm sorry this is so painful for you but I can't change who I am.

JANE. You expect me to though, don't you?

*Silence.*

TOM, *carrying a suitcase has come into the room unnoticed.*

You don't give a damn if you never see Heather Cottage again, do you?

PAUL. That's not true.

JANE. You faked it with me. You've faked it with the children and I bet you faked it through every holiday we ever had here.

PAUL. Jane, stop it. That's not true. You know how much they meant to me.

JANE. I don't. I don't know.

PAUL. We can share the cottage.

JANE. Oh yes, Paul, that would suit you fine, wouldn't it? But you don't own it.

PAUL. Well, neither do you.

JANE. It belongs to the children.

TOM. And we want to keep it. For all of us. Just stop fighting. The whole point of coming down here was to make things better, not worse.

*Silence.*

PAUL. So: we're decided. We sell the house and buy two flats.

JANE. There'll be a lot of hard work making it all happen.

PAUL. But, in principle, it's the answer?

JANE. Agreed.

PAUL. And Tom shares his time between us.

JANE. Yes.

PAUL. Good.

JANE. But I want you to live under the same roof as Alice and me.

*Beat.*

PAUL. This is all about what Tom wants?

JANE. No. I mean it. On that I put my foot down.

PAUL. This is ridiculous, why?

JANE. It's a big world out there with lots of very nasty things in it and I'm not sure Tom is quite ready –

PAUL. What nasty things will he find with me, // that he won't find with you?

*Beat.*

So that's it. Because you feel strongly then I have to give up my share of Tom.

JANE. Give him up. He's not a chattel in a divorce case. He's a fifteen-year-old boy who's still very innocent in lots of ways. He's vulnerable and impressionable and in case you've forgotten, he's our son.

PAUL. Oh Christ Almighty, what's that supposed to mean?

JANE. Just use your imagination. I don't suppose celibacy is going to figure greatly in your new-found bachelor status, is it?

PAUL. Oh don't be so insufferably priggish.

JANE. This new flat isn't exactly going to be a family-friendly area, is it?

PAUL. Oh change the fucking record!

JANE. Don't swear at me. You have poisoned everything you have ever touched. You've driven us apart. Your daughter loathes the ground you walk on. And now you're trying to steal my son.

PAUL. I have had this. I have had this up to here.

*He slams out of the cottage.*

*Silence.*

TOM *in the course of this latest outburst of hostilities has curled up in a ball in a corner of the room with his hands over his ears, trying to shut out the fury.* JANE *sits at the table, silent tears streaming down her face oblivious. Maybe her head on her arms.* TOM *gets up very quietly and picks up up a suitcase he brought into the room earlier and puts it on the chair opposite* JANE. *Then he comes around to* JANE*'s side of the table and gives her a hug.*

TOM. Don't cry Mum.

*Pause.*

I think Dad was wrong not to tell you from the start he was gay but he's still my Dad and I love him just the same because mostly that's what you do, isn't it? You love your Dad whatever.

JANE. I don't want you not to love him Tom.

*Beat.*

TOM. You know, you and Dad rowing has always been so scary. Ever since I can remember. I used to think it was the end of the world. Sometimes I'd wake up and hear you both and go crying to Alice // thinking it was my fault and she'd explain.

JANE. // Oh Tom. I'm so sorry.

*Pause.*

JANE. OK Tom. Look. If you still want to stay with your Dad when we've sold up and found our two flats, we'll give it a try. A trial period. You can always change your mind.

TOM. Oh Mum, that is so cool, that's brilliant.

*Beat.*

TOM. When Alice comes to stay with you will you let her boyfriend stay over?

JANE. Does she have a boyfriend?

TOM. I don't know.

JANE. I think I'll wait and decide when I meet him in the flesh.

TOM. What if it was a girl?

JANE. What do you mean?

TOM. Suppose she was going out with a girl?

JANE. I think it would depend on what sort of person the girl turned out to be. I don't have a problem with gay people, Tom. I just never bargained on sharing my life with a man with two very different souls.

TOM. OK, Mum. That's cool.

*Pause.*

I'm going to go and find Dad, and tell him it's sorted.

*Silence.*

JANE *comes round to where the suitcase is and opens it. Inside is a dog-eared teddy bear and the badger costume we saw in Scene Three. It has a big card on it with a message.* JANE *takes it out of the suitcase and reads it*

JANE. Brill Badger Rules OK.

*Fade to black.*


### Scene Twenty

JANE *and* ANNA. *Somewhere neutral.*

ANNA. Extraordinary.

JANE. What would you have done?

ANNA. I don't know. I really don't. Absolutely extraordinary.

JANE. It wasn't as if you could've joined the wives with gay husbands' club.

ANNA. Is there one?

JANE. I'm damn sure there ought to be. It's been going on for centuries.

ANNA. It's extraordinary.

JANE. Isn't it?

ANNA. I had absolutely no idea.

JANE. You weren't meant to.

ANNA. Paul's such a macho man.

JANE. Do you think?

ANNA. Yes. And very attractive.

JANE. To both sexes.

ANNA. Poor you.

JANE. Do you know the thing I really found attractive about him?

ANNA. What?

JANE. His lack of machismo.

*Pause.*

ANNA. How did you put up with all the . . .

JANE. What?

ANNA. I was going to say rejection.

JANE. It wasn't really me he was rejecting.

*Beat.*

ANNA. Not like Jeremy. But then he's just a bastard.

JANE. I'm sorry.

ANNA. It's probably for the best: J.J. couldn't stand him.

JANE. How is J.J. by the way?

ANNA. His Dad tells me he's wonderful with the baby.

JANE. You're not jealous are you?

ANNA. Not in the slightest.

*Pause.*

JANE. You are, aren't you?

*Beat.* ANNA *smiles*

Extraordinary. I can hardly believe I'm saying this but talking to you is actually a bit of a relief.

ANNA. Do you think it runs in families? I mean do you think it's genetic in some way or other?

JANE. What?

ANNA. Being attracted to the same sex.

JANE (*beat*). No. I don't think anybody or anything makes you gay. Or straight.

*Beat.*

Be not afraid of gayness. Some are born gay, some achieve gaiety, and some have gay men thrust upon 'em.

ANNA. Goodness. (*Giggles.*) Well. Que sera sera.

Do you really want to go off and do this now?

JANE. I don't know. I just wanted you to go with me. You can tell me what you think. It was your idea!

ANNA. It was just a suggestion. I don't want you to be doing // something that

JANE (*interrupts*). I'm not sure if I want electrolysis or not but whatever I decide I'll be doing for me.

ANNA. Because Paul never noticed?

JANE. He doesn't matter.

ANNA. Of course.

JANE. I'm on my own and I'm doing it for me.

ANNA. You're not necessarily going to stay like that.

JANE. I wouldn't give a damn if I wasn't touched sexually ever again. It's not even on my list let alone near the top.

I've been on my own for years I'd just like to feel good about myself for me.

ANNA. This calls for a toast. One for the road.

*She takes out her silver flask. Pours out two drinks.*

Well, what's it to be?

JANE. How about . . . To being oneself.

*They drink.*

ANNA. Shall we go, then?

JANE. Yes, let's go.

*The End.*

**A Nick Hern Book**

*The Maths Tutor* first published in Great Britain in 2003
as a paperback original by Nick Hern Books, 14 Larden Road,
London W3 7ST, in association with the Hampstead Theatre,
London, and Birmingham Repertory Theatre

*The Maths Tutor* copyright © 2003 by Clare McIntyre

Clare McIntyre has asserted her moral right to be identified
as the author of this work

Typeset by Country Setting, Kingsdown, Kent CT14 8ES
Printed and bound in Great Britain by Bookmarque, Croydon,
Surrey

A CIP catalogue record for this book is available from
the British Library

ISBN 1 85459 766 3

**CAUTION**   All rights whatsoever in this play are strictly reserved.
Requests to reproduce the text in whole or in part should be
addressed to the publisher.

**Amateur Performing Rights**   Applications for performance
by amateurs, including readings and excerpts, should be addressed
to the Performing Rights Manager, Nick Hern Books, 14 Larden
Road, London W3 7ST, *fax* +44(020)8735 0250, *e-mail*
info@nickhernbooks.demon.co.uk, except as follows:

*Australia*   Dominie Drama, 8 Cross Street, Brookvale 2100,
*fax* (2) 9905 5209, *e-mail* dominie@dominie.com.au

*New Zealand*   Play Bureau, PO Box 420, New Plymouth,
*fax* (6)753 2150, *e-mail* play.bureau.nz@xtra.co.nz

*United States of America and Canada*   The Agency – as below

**Professional Performing Rights**   Application for performance
by professionals in any medium and in any language throughout
the world and for amateur and stock rights in USA and Canada
should be addressed to the author's agent, The Agency, 24 Pottery
Lane, Holland Park, London W11 4LZ, *tel.* (020) 7727 1346,
*fax* (020) 7727 9037

No performance of any kind may be given unless a licence has
been obtained. Applications should be made before rehearsals
begin. Publication of this play does not necessarily indicate its
availability for amateur performance.